1500
PROVERBS
and
COMMENTS

Extracted from the Journal of a
Christian Highwayman

RAYMOND B. DUNN

authorHOUSE®

AuthorHouse™ UK
1663 Liberty Drive
Bloomington, IN 47403 USA
www.authorhouse.co.uk
Phone: UK TFN: 0800 0148641 (Toll Free inside the UK)
UK Local: 02036 956322 (+44 20 3695 6322 from outside the UK)

Published by AuthorHouse 10/16/2020

ISBN: 978-1-6655-8093-9 (sc)
ISBN: 978-1-6655-8094-6 (hc)
ISBN: 978-1-6655-8092-2 (e)

Ray opens his personal journal to share 1500 proverbs, sayings and comments gathered while walking along the Christian Highway during the years 2006 to 2020.

ABOUT THE AUTHOR

Ray was born in Sheffield in 1944. At the age of four he was diagnosed with asthma; this crippling disease dominated his early life. Recovery and survival meant spending most of his childhood away from home, where at one convalescent home he almost died, not through this illness, but through fooling around in an open-air swimming pool. He testifies that at the critical moment, as he struggled, he felt the hand of an angel lift his head above the surface, which saved his life.

Married with three children, and now five grandchildren, Ray has had a number of jobs in industry; first making parts for the aero division of Rolls Royce. Later, after retraining, as a Project Engineer in the food industry, before being made redundant aged forty-nine. Unable to get another job, he went to Art College, after which he started his own ceramics business as a potter – before his eventual retirement to serve as a shepherd to his small flock of Black Welsh Mountain sheep. Ray also keeps bees; he currently has five hives.

He has lived in the lovely Yorkshire Dales (as a boy)

in the city of Sheffield, and now in retirement, with his wife Margaret in the beautiful mountains of Snowdonia.

Ray has been a devoted Christian ever since the 2nd November 1962. He was in bed reading a Christian book called "The Day Christ Died" by Jim Bishop. Reading of how Jesus Christ, gave His life to die a cruel death on the cross to save him, Ray broke down, wept, and promised God that if He would help him, then he would try to behave himself from thereon. At which point he became aware someone was standing at the foot of his bed, but he was so scared, he dived under the covers, eventually to fall asleep still clutching the book. Ray is convinced the same angel that saved his life, when a boy, revealed himself again at the foot of his bed at his decision to start a new life following Jesus Christ. Thus, Ray set off along the Highway following Jesus, and by keeping a journal, has been able to recall, easily, much of the truth he has learnt.

INTRODUCTION

"Precept upon precept, line upon line..." is the structured, secure way that God educates His children. Tossing the Bible to us, expecting we educate ourselves by reading it, or by heeding the advice of other people, are not His ways – lest we fail to grow up in His image and likeness.

When teaching His children, God does everything possible to teach them right from wrong, and it helps enormously if we maintain a good relationship with Him. And with a good relationship, how could we not rejoice when the King travels with us, for then the journey alone is worth it.

One alternative description of *"precept upon precept, line upon line"*, are the proverbs, thoughts and advice we encounter in our walk with Jesus that stop us in our tracks and influence our lives for the better. Keeping a journal can help recall such welcome breadcrumbs more easily.

Highwaymen will find the 'Highway of Holiness' to be a narrow path alongside a crocodile-infested river, not a smooth, three-lane, tarmacked-motorway to heaven.

For the children of Israel, Canaan lay at the other side of a great and terrible wilderness. Their journey to the Promised Land could never have been a comfortable, leisurely and pleasurable journey and neither could ours. Except for the Manna and a flowing-spring provided by God, the wilderness cannot support life. Walking such a highway requires determination; stay close to the Shepherd – Jesus, and do not look back!

This book, the fourth in the 'Sharing My Bread" series, is the result of reviewing the *precept upon precept and the line upon line*, as recorded in this highwayman's journal.

Note: All Scriptural references are from the NKJ version of the Bible, published by Thomas Nelson.

1500 PROVERBS AND COMMENTS FROM A CHRISTIAN HIGHWAYMAN

GOD is good! Everything He thinks, says and does is very good! Nothing bad comes from Him, nor does He applaud it.

2   God is light! He spoke and His word flooded chaos and the blackest-void, with light. In His presence darkness cannot abide.

3   *Everything* our senses detect around us *is* His spoken Word – absolutely everything! This must be so because there was nothing here before He spoke.

4   God is genuine; He never tells lies or deceives. There are many opinions and much advice, but to be sure of finding genuine, life-giving truth, one should seek only Him for the answers to life's important questions.

5   God is love; therefore, despite what others may say about Him, He hates no one.

6   God is merciful; He loves to forgive, eager even, and never requires or desires revenge, but to benefit from His mercy, one must repent from sin and humbly turn to Him.

7   God is righteous! Righteousness has a restraining influence on everything He says and does; this makes Him very predictable.

8 God is; everything else is, only because He is!

9 God has no need to defend Himself, or His throne.

10 God is generous; therefore, by having His nature, all His children should grow to become generous.

11 Those who grow up respecting and forgiving their neighbour will spend eternity with Him.

12 God respects our authority; He expects us to respect His.

13 Nothing we can do, learn of, or achieve, compensates for not knowing God.

14 To know Him is eternal life, and to understand Him is a realistic ambition.

15 Being in the presence of God exceeds by far being anywhere else.

16 And being right with Him exceeds by far being right with anyone else.

17 Throughout eternity, the One Supreme God administers His authority via His spoken Word.

18 God communicates His will through what He says, never through gestures.

19 In character, God never changes, but His glory increases continually.

20 The underlying principle of uncleanness is that in spite of what we may think, and what we may claim, or what we may do, while in such a condition, the holy God is not among us.

2 Anyone having God at a distance is in grave danger.

2 His good news message, about His Son Jesus Christ, is an invitation for people to turn from chaos darkness and death, to wash clean from it, and follow His Son to His kingdom of truth, light and life. And on the way, the more we get to know Him, the more we will love Him.

3   But our words alone, spoken or sung, are insufficient proof of our love.
4   Jesus Christ is everything of value; everybody is nobody without Him,
5   Everywhere is nowhere without Him, and everything is nothing without Him!
6   Not many people realise this, and let other things crowd Him out of their lives.
7   Father God loves his children; He desires a close relationship with them.
8   Close relationships always result in both parties getting to know each other; for His children, growing up to know their heavenly Father should be inevitable.
9   However, any relationship must involve communication; before God can communicate with us, He must first get our attention; if our mind is on other things, then He does not have our attention.
10 Father God loves His children and provides life-giving bread for them.
11 His children prove their love for Him and His bread, by seeking Him for it.
12 Individuals cannot dwell peaceably together unless they agree.
13 Therefore, to dwell peaceably with us, God must come to an agreement with us.
14 The love vows between a man and his wife, and between God and men, are effectively identical. Both relationships include faithfulness; neither includes violence, physical or verbal, and both should give of themselves to please the other.
15 Righteousness determines that those outside the law, but who keep it, are right, whereas those who live within the law, but disregard its principles, are wrong.

16 Couples promise each other love, care and faithfulness, but many break their promises, with or without the Marriage Certificate.

17 Many who make promises to God, break them too, thinking it does not matter, and no one will notice.

18 Neither God's Law nor a Marriage Certificate guarantees we will keep our promises to each other.

19 Therefore, before judging anyone, take into account, who is and who is not keeping their vows, rather than who has, and who has not got a Certificate, or who does and who does not go to church.

20 Likewise, observe the behaviour, rather than just the words of your neighbour. This is wise, not disrespectful.

3 God provided *"The sun to rule the day"* to give of what it has to benefit those beneath it.

2 King Jesus reigns over all; His example of the word *rule* was to willingly give Himself for the benefit of all beneath Him.

3 From God's viewpoint, the word *rule* means *to shepherd,* not govern.

4 God instructed Adam to rule over the earth; therefore, Adam was meant to serve and benefit all beneath him, not use and abuse it.

5 A shepherd's responsibilities are to lead, teach, provide for, and protect the flock, not the other way round; all shepherds need to heed this.

6 Ever since Adam, the word 'rule' has been misused.

7 Through Ezekiel, the Holy Spirit rebukes shepherds that feed and clothe themselves from those whom they should be feeding and clothing.

8 Adam failed and shepherds fail, but by refusing to feed off those kneeling at His feet, Jesus succeeded.

9   God, in speaking to the woman, put her under the *rule* of her man.

10 Using the word *rule*, God was saying to the woman, that her man would lead, teach, provide for and protect her; all men need to heed this.

11 Also, that she must never again follow anyone else's advice, nor accept tuition, provisions or protection offered by another; all wives need to heed this.

12 Today, more women than men may be attending church, but those assuming more women than men will make it into heaven, could be mistaken.

13 Many women attending church, supporting charities and doing good works, *are* devout, but devout to whom?

14 God commanded the woman to submit her will to that of her man.

15 And at her wedding, a wife promises devotion to her husband, not to the pastor, a church or any organisation; she is not her own, just as men belong to Jesus; they are not their own either.

16 A wife may cringe and squirm at the idea of total submission to the will of her husband, but her man has a greater responsibility to God, for her.

17 Far more men cringe, squirm and rebel, at the idea of total submission to Jesus, than wives do towards their husbands.

18 While remaining obedient to God, Adam and Eve enjoyed paradise; all they did to lose *everything* was take someone else's advice.

19 And by seeking advice from other people, we leave ourselves open to making the same mistake.

20 Each time we do this, we risk heeding the voice of the serpent while thinking it is the voice of a friend.

4 Leadership is lordship! Leaders are shepherds; your shepherd is your lord, but sheep that do not have ears to hear, will not understand this.

2 Men may reproduce themselves spiritually, as well as physically.

3 Leaders and teachers, in all fields, reproduce themselves through their disciples with the bread they feed to them.

4 Disciplined followers, grow to reflect their tutors in what they believe, in what they say, and in how they behave.

5 Therefore, choose and follow only the Son, whom God, who is above all, anointed as Leader.

6 Ideally, those representing Jesus should respond in word and deed in the same way as He did.

7 Do not heed or follow anyone who does not teach and do the same works that Jesus did.

8 Place the education of children under the care of unrighteous people, and they will teach them unrighteousness.

9 Initially, the unrighteous tutor will teach about sin, then tolerance of it, then acceptance of it, and finally encourage it; pray to God that they never get to enforce it; here, something about a millstone hung around the neck and deep water, comes to mind.

10 God seeded this Creation with mature creatures. To bear fruit and multiply, a certain amount of maturity is essential.

11 *"Then God blessed them, and God said to them, 'Be fruitful and multiply...'"*

12 A blessing is not necessarily a feeling, but rather God's permission to multiply, to experience increase and prosperity.

13 Creation was a one-off, from thereon, the creation had to reproduce after its own kind, but rather than being mature, *'their own kind'* were born wild.

14 At birth, all creatures are wild, untamed, ignorant, and in need of instruction.

15 Wild creatures are lawless, a law unto themselves. The instruction was for Adam to subdue them, to tame them.

16 By presenting them with the food they like, it is always possible to tame wild creatures.

17 But even God cannot tame men who have no taste for His bread.

18 Fantasy and lies keep people immature because they are not food for growth.

19 One may live while believing fairy stories, fiction and fantasy, but one never grows up while doing so.

20 We truly are what we consume, spiritually as well as naturally.

5 A father has nothing to be proud of if his family is intelligent, healthy and wealthy, but starving spiritually.

2 Men will answer to God for where they lead their family, what they teach them, how they provide for them, and how well they protect them.

3 Religious leaders, of all faiths and titles will face the same rigorous examination regarding the health and safety of the sheep that follow them.

4 We will all give an account for the *bread* we gather and feed to those for whom we are responsible.

5 Eating the bread of God is the way to grow up in His image and His likeness.

6 No other bread meets the stringent nutritional standard or results in such a glorious reward.

7 The bread that God offers us is genuine truth; the bread offered to us by other people is second-hand and often questionable.

8 God offers life-nourishing food to the individual, as well as providing a list of important laws essential for lawless people.

9 To mature, we need to absorb the truth; unless we absorb the truth, we will never grow up no matter how long we live, or how long we remain Christians.

10 Truth is reality; it is food for growth; in fact, spiritual growth is the process of continually gathering and feeding on truth.

11 Curiosity about what another thinks is not a hunger for truth.

12 Curiosity makes one vulnerable; therefore, seek only Jesus for the truth He offers!

13 *Information* is not the truth being spoken of here. The strange thing about truth is that it is not just information; therefore, one cannot give or receive it as though it were.

14 We avoid deception by finding out for ourselves what God has to say, not by listening to what others say He has to say.

15 We are not orphans; God does not abandon His children to grow up on their own through reading books and listening to the instructions and advice other people give.

16 Christians travel the world to hear the words of a preacher, unaware that the Spirit of truth is by their side, eager to lead, teach and feed them His bread.

17 His bread, as well as being precious, is also dangerous.

18 History shows that if one mentions His bread in the wrong ear, then opposition, hatred and violence are likely to follow; saints have not been safe from this, even within Christianity.

19 "We are what we eat!" Accepting the truth, chewing it over and digesting it, means it will become part of us. The same is true of trash.

20 It is disrespectful to approach God for help while having plan 'B' tucked in our back pocket.

6 To distribute rewards to obedient souls worthy of entering His kingdom, God must identify them.

2 To distinguish such people, from the countless multitudes that only mention His name, there is a simple test. He tells us what to do, and then watches to see if we do it.

3 *"Then* the LORD *said to Moses, 'Behold, I will rain bread from heaven for you. And the people shall go out and gather a certain quota every day, that I may test them, whether they will walk in My law or not. And it shall be on the sixth day that they shall prepare what they bring in, and it shall be twice as much as they gather daily...' "*

4 God scatters His bread all around our *camp* for six days; the Sabbath should be spent thanking Him for it.

5 Before sunrise, seek and gather His bread before it evaporates in the heat of the day.

6 Few tests are as simple to describe, and yet few tests have proven themselves so difficult to overcome.

7 They called that bread *"Manna"*, which translated means, *"What is it?"* an apt name for something yet to be revealed; that was miracle bread, but it was not heavenly bread.

8 Believing what we read in the Bible, is of no use if we are misunderstanding what it is saying.

9 The bread from God is Jesus; His word is the truth provided for us by the Holy Spirit. Therefore, we too

can ask, 'What is it?' and only as He feeds it to us will we find out.

10 Because we are what we eat, we can grow up to become like God only by eating His bread.

11 Consume only what the world offers to us, and we will grow to become like the world; everyone chasing qualifications, jobs, and enjoying the entertainment provided by the world, should consider this.

12 We show that we love God, not by our words, or by our labours, but by our obedience to Him.

13 His test sorts out, not only those who are obedient, from those who are not, but it also reveals to what degree.

14 Some men gather; some men expect others to gather for them.

15 Sunday mornings seem to be a popular time to sample someone else's bread.

16 There must be some difference between the words when God speaks them, and the same words when men speak them, but what?

17 All preachers *need* the answer, before standing up to speak for God.

18 We are not disciples of Jesus if we seek advice from and follow the instructions of others.

19 How many Christians, while thinking they are disciples of Jesus, are just students of other men?

20 How many Christians, while thinking they are His Bride, are unfaithful in serving and following the advice of others?

7 God Most High is the Saviour, not the destroyer.

2 His power is not in the ability to destroy, any fool can do that, and they do!

3 God is the Creator, the Saviour, the Deliverer, the Healer the Provider, the Teacher, and the Repairer, all equally good.

4 He is Almighty when designing, creating, building, saving, delivering, loving, healing, making, pleasing, repairing, comforting, multiplying, sharing, supporting, helping and giving.

5 Everything God does is perfect in every way, so why should He destroy any of it?

6 There is no skill in destroying things, no artistic gifting and no beauty.

7 Death, decay and chaos are not beautiful, well designed or useful.

8 The only thing death, decay and chaos can do, is reduce people and things to nothing.

9 By misunderstanding God's justice, one man can become quite capable of administering pain and deliberate destruction to another.

10 Warnings, judgements, curses and destructions specified in Scripture, as coming from God, are not threats of what He will do to the disobedient, but rather prophecies of what will happen to them by another.

11 It is far too easy to attribute human characteristics to God.

12 Vengeance is a particularly spiteful characteristic of human nature.

13 Vengeful judgements come easily to man; therefore, thinking this righteous, he attributes it as also coming from God.

14 Repeating what we hear, without proof that it is true, is careless, especially when talking about God – lest we bear false witness against Him.

15 People, who do not truly know Him, occasionally testify about Him doing some terrible things.

16 Without understanding, and being unaware of the serpent, many blame God when trouble strikes.

17 To ensure we only tell the truth, and to avoid blasphemy, we should *only* testify of our own experiences with God.

18 Violence occurs neither at His command nor with His approval, although many testimonies contradict this, but today is the day for salvation; Judgement Day is later.

19 Jesus came to reveal the true character of His Father God, and to make an open show of the devil.

20 Our determination to follow Jesus must be greater than our enemy's determination to stop us.

8 The Lord God in heaven is Truth, He is Light and He is Life, without Him these features do not exist anywhere.

2 Therefore, if we reject Him, then we reject truth, light and life, and stay chaotic, in darkness, dead.

3 Without God, there can only ever be chaos, darkness, and death.

4 Paraphrased, Moses said, *"Hear O Israel, the LORD our God, the LORD is one; we have no other!"*

5 Sadly, for most of the time, they had several, as have many who are called by His name today.

6 To get to know God, spending time alone with Him is essential.

7 To know Him, one must walk with Him, eat with Him, sleep with Him, laugh with Him and cry with Him.

8 Spending time with Him is the only way to get to know Him. Listening to sermons describing Him and His ways is just listening to gossip! Most sermons are just gossip.

9 We must first learn what is true before being able to reject what is false. If we accept a lie, believing it is

true, then, when presented with the truth, we will reject it as being a lie.

10 Beware; men can believe a lie, and in all sincerity and with great passion, assure us that it is the absolute truth.

11 Our sense of smell is the radar system we have that forewarns us of both good and bad things before we approach and partake of them.

12 Spiritual Discernment is a gift from God that is comparable to our natural sense of smell.

13 If the spiritual gift of discernment is as useful as its natural counterpart, then surely we should all desire to possess it, and if we already have it, to use it.

14 Do we have a spiritual sense of smell keen enough to warn us of dangerous places, harmful things, of deceitful people and false doctrine, before they have a chance to infect us?

15 Spiritually, do we give off a sweet, *heavenly* scent, or a foul *earthy* stench?

16 Is it possible, with just a spiritual sniff, to know that the person with whom we are speaking has been muck spreading?

17 Could sloppy doctrine, gossip and lies, equal bad breath?

18 Does the spiritual poo that we trod in, while revelling in the world, still cling to our shoes as we walk into church?

19 Does the smell of it follow us everywhere, and do we leave traces of it wherever we have been?

20 Do we screw up our faces at fresh, life-giving bread, while sat happily chewing on TV vomit?

9 Moses was raised in Pharaoh's household and in his ways.

2 When Moses killed the Egyptian and fled from Pharaoh into the wilderness, he was full of Pharaoh and his ways.

3 No man, using the methods taught by Pharaoh, can do the work of God.

4 Moses set out thinking he was capable of *ruling* his people *in* Egypt, but God wanted him to *lead* them *out* of it; think about that!

5 It is both disrespectful and foolish to laugh and joke at the bedside of sick people.

6 We may think we are cheering them up, but how do they feel after we have walked away?

7 Are they still sick, in pain and heading for the same destination?

8 An amusing, entertaining gospel shows disrespect towards Jesus, who suffered and died painfully to provide it.

9 Preachers face the sick, suffering and dying each time they stand to lecture their flock. Can they provide what they preach? Does their power match their words?

10 Like laughter in the sickroom, sermons are not the place for jokes.

11 Out of respect for people, and the leaders' people choose, Jesus teaches no one; no one that is, except His disciples.

12 Men do not teach disciples of Jesus; He does!

13 The fact that God only does what is right, means His Son only does what is right; this limits Their involvement with unrepentant, sinful people.

14 Unless it is accompanied by the gospel, God cannot bless those in sin, without encouraging them to remain there.

15 Turning from our sin unto God is the first step towards receiving any blessing from Him.

16 God does not afflict His children, but He has enemies who do.

17 While ever we have an evil adversary stalking our footsteps, then sufferings of one sort or another are inevitable.

18 One thing is sure, Jesus will heal and set us free from anything that prevents us from entering His kingdom; after that, the enemy is free to do everything in his power to get us out again.

19 The best and safest way to enjoy our Christian life is for the individual to decide what he or she would enjoy doing, and then to do it, for Jesus, with Jesus.

20 Invite Jesus into your life and He will invite you into His; in fact, inviting Jesus into your life is the *only* way for Him to invite you into His.

10 We serve those whom we obey. Muslims follow Mohamed, Jews follow Moses, and while ever they do, neither can follow Jesus Christ, but those who call themselves 'Christian' follow many leaders.

2 While ever the devil can keep God's people following pastors, teachers and leaders, he prevents them from following Jesus.

3 And while ever the devil can divert God's children from private prayer, into praying in public, he can discourage God from answering.

4 Jesus taught that a servant can serve only one master, but I know Christians do not accept this because

they accept alternative pastors, teachers and leaders, sometimes many!

5 Most Christians believe they are disciples of Jesus, but true disciples of Jesus are very rare.

6 For the Christian to desire a pastor, is for him or her to reject Jesus as their pastor.

7 Can children choose their parents? Democracy has a serious flaw – men choose their leaders!

8 The kingdom of God is not a democracy. Is it wise for God's children to pick and choose who should lead and teach them?

9 Bought by His blood, we belong to Jesus; can we follow or cast our vote for another? Belonging to Him, do we have a vote to cast?

10 Voting for a leader, other than Jesus, is being unfaithful to the King, the King whom God chose and anointed to lead us.

11 Cast your pearls before swine; cast your vote for an unrighteous, blind politician, and then watch and wait as he or she turns to oppose you.

12 The politicians Christians choose, show no respect towards God, His Son or the Law He gave us; instead, for your vote, they will show more respect for unrighteousness and foreign gods.

13 Each consecutive government has discarded God's Law to introduce theirs.

14 Once Bible-based, our laws now face the opposite direction to become almost anti-Christian.

15 The politician leaves the nation in a worse state than when he arrived – not so Jesus!

16 Today, Britain lives in the afterglow of a Christian era that is quickly fading.

17 Continue choosing men, secular and religious, to lead us, and it will result in our prosperous, persecution-free environment disappearing completely.

18 Israel demanded a king; God said to Samuel, *"Heed the voice of the people ... they have not rejected you, but they have rejected Me that I should not reign over them... However, warn them of the ways of kings."* Selah!

19 Christian take note, who is the bigger fool, the blind man who offers to lead, or the one who can see, choosing to follow him?

20 Following blind leaders is not wise. Stay faithful to Jesus your Redeemer; vote for Him as your only Shepherd every morning and follow Him each day.

11 Presumptuous people read of Jesus commissioning His disciples and assume He was speaking to them. It is unwise to harbour presumption.

2 Jesus filled the gap between Him saying *"Come follow Me"* and *"Go, disciple the nations"* with perfect and intense tuition.

3 Presumption in this area is the reason for ineffective preachers.

4 For all practical reasons, the word *faith* simply means the same as the word *confidence*.

5 What weakens *confidence* more than anything else, if not failure?

6 Presumptuous preachers can destroy people's confidence in the Almighty very quickly.

7 Righteousness is not something you either have or have not; righteousness is more like a colour that varies in intensity, or like a foreign language you are learning.

8 Jesus, being the express image of His Father, reveals His brilliance and His righteousness, and He speaks His language like a natural.

9 Jesus said, *"The thief does not come except to steal and to kill and to destroy."* Recognise his signature, judge covetousness, persecution, and destructive events, correctly.

10 The enemy is quite capable of providing carrots; he offered Jesus all the kingdoms of the world, so he is not short of carrots.

11 Carrots work most effectively on people who like carrots.

12 Covetousness is the desire for carrots, especially the carrots belonging to other people.

13 The warning to all desiring carrots is that some carrots are much easier to acquire than they are to discard.

14 Some who are unfaithful to Jesus, do not abandon their relationship with Him; instead, secretively or brazenly, they keep lovers on the side.

15 The message of the *true* prophet is to avoid coming judgement and therefore, is usually a call to repentance; people don't like him; he gets lots of frowns and criticism.

16 The message of the *false* prophet is soothing, comforting and uplifting, people smile, greet and speak well of him.

17 Only superficial authority is given to children, it directly relates to their age, experience and how responsible they are proving themselves to be.

18 Men fail their sons, by not teaching them how to get answers to their questions directly from God.

19 Once away from parental supervision, they then ask their questions of others, and so are misled.

20 Learning about God is not the same as getting to know Him; parents, pastors and churches fail children and their flock by not stressing this.

12 Regarding truth, ask your questions only of Jesus.
2 Regarding truth, ask question of others only after Jesus has given you the answer.
3 Not knowing the truth, makes it too easy to accept a lie.
4 However, asking questions of sleepy, uninterested people disturbs them, likewise religious people in a rut; it confuses and irritates them; they lose their peace and friction is then likely.
5 But asking children questions will awaken inquisitiveness; excited, they will then seek answers.
6 The degree to which God's children are excited by Him, and their response to His word, shows to what degree they love Him.
7 Taking the advice of Jesus above the advice of all others is proof that we value Him, His Word and His way, above all others.
8 By gathering and analysing the effects, it should be possible to diagnose a cause; doctors do this as they examine symptoms in their patients.
9 If we reverse the procedure and examine a cause, then we should be able to forecast an effect.
10 We could label the one method that uses hindsight, *diagnosis* and the other that uses foresight, *prophecy*.
11 We could accept the word repent, to mean, *on reflection, change direction*.
12 Being in the kingdom of God is neither sitting idle in a church warming a pew nor is it working hard in a church polishing it.
13 Once inside Canaan, the Israelites saw themselves as having arrived; they had made it! For them, there remained no other Promised Land.

14 Joining a church, convinces many that they also have arrived; they have become a Christian, and think they are safe inside the kingdom of God.

15 The preservation of Job's life was the only limitation God set for his enemy, everything else that Job had, Satan was able to steal, kill and destroy it.

16 Job had no other alternative but to grit his teeth, sit out the assault, the accusations of his friends, and the silence from heaven, and trust in the God who hides Himself in thick clouds.

17 Some who suffer sickness, infirmity or persecution, have no one else, except Job, as an example. Our only consolation is that faithfulness pays off in the end – the end is seeing God as He really is!

18 There is an immense difference between learning about God and getting to know Him.

19 I say again: the fundamental problem, with learning about Him, is that it is reliant upon information supplied by other people; this is no better than listening to gossip.

20 And if we are genuine about wanting to know God, then learning about Him through gossip is very unreliable, and many sermons are just gossip.

13 Both naturally and spiritually, we are what we eat!

2 Consider the grass, it gets all its nourishment from the soil, which must mean that grass consists entirely of the elements and nutrients found in soil.

3 Sheep eat grass, and little else, which must mean that sheep consist entirely of the elements and nutrients found in grass.

4 Therefore, technically, if not in appearance and behaviour, grass and sheep are just an extension of soil.

5 The fact that the soil, the grass and the sheep differ only in appearance and behaviour is amazing.

6 As remarkable as the trans-formation from soil to grass to sheep is, it is not as important as the realisation that whatever eats only grass, or sheep, can only ever be an extension of soil; think about that!

7 Because this means, if I consume only what this world has to offer me, then the soil, the grass, the sheep and I, would remain virtually the same thing, just dirt.

8 Those desiring to leave this world and go to heaven must prepare themselves by becoming part of heaven; we accomplish this by eating what comes from heaven.

9 Regarding heavenly food, man has always been a *hunter-gatherer*. If successful in his hunting and gathering, then nourished with heavenly food, he will grow to become heavenly, which is essential if he desires to go there.

10 Moses fasted forty days and nights on the mountain of God. Jesus also fasted throughout the forty days He was in the wilderness.

11 Questioning why they fasted forty days is pointless because such places have neither food nor water. Fasting is not an option in a wilderness.

12 To walk into a wilderness means to turn our backs on the world, and walk to our death – the death of our old nature.

13 God finds the slow and unskilled, but reliable and obedient, far more helpful than self-confident, clever achievers, who enjoy doing their own thing, rather than what He asks of them.

14 Respectful people, even if unskilled, are far more desirable company than those who are competent, but disrespectful.

15 Welcome disrespectful people into a respectful kingdom, and they will take it over and turn it into a kingdom full of disrespectful people.

16 Neither God nor His Son *uses* people, especially not His children. Using people for one's own benefit is disrespectful and God is never disrespectful.

17 Before creating anything, God first decides whether He is going to have a relationship with it; likewise, we should never *use* or *misuse* anything with which we could have a relationship.

18 God seems to prefer and select the most unlikely people for the most outstanding jobs.

19 Often, unlikely and incapable people desire those outstanding jobs, and God likes to please His children.

20 Giving of what we have to those in need until it runs out is a heavenly principle.

14 According to the proverb, *"Among a multitude of words sin is not lacking."* We can apply similar carelessness to *"speaking words without understanding"*.

2 Along with the preacher, all speakers and teachers produce a profusion of words; they are all particularly vulnerable to this fault.

3 Consider this: If we build God a house and furnish it, we can then move Him out of our simple dwelling and into His elaborate one.

4 From thereon we can visit Him anytime it is convenient for us.

5 Confining God to a special house is very convenient for those unwilling for Him to live in theirs.

6 Religious men can treasure, as holy, the houses they build, while persecuting the true dwelling place of God – His children.

7   If human nature is unsuccessful in diverting the convert back into the world, then all sorts of external things will join forces with it, trying to achieve the same.

8   If these do not work, then the enemy will send people with religious projects, good ideas and attractive offers as a distraction.

9   Such, along with countless other external things, will unite with our human nature and attempt to divert us back into the world.

10 If this powerful, yet subtle combination fails to distract and divert us, then others will appear seeking to control us.

11 In seeking to displace God and become our masters, these people will demand our attention, attempt to keep our lives busy, or else will try to rearrange our priorities.

12 There is something odd about one man asking another to open, or close a meeting with prayer; it is a habit, a social nicety, nothing to do with God.

13 Leaders use others to enhance their programme and use prayer in several ways to control meetings.

14 The phrase, "Let us pray!" silences the people to begin the leader's programme.

15 And other leaders, who have other things they would rather be doing, use prayer as a tool to close meetings. Such prayers are dead before they hit the walls.

16 The prophet, or the preacher, is only God's second-best way of communicating with His people.

17 Primarily, it is through a loving, one-to-one relationship.

18 Every man represents his master; we are not 'lights' for Jesus if He is not our Shepherd.

19 Many Christians believe they are following Jesus, when in reality they follow those who lead, those who lead, their leader.

20 Christian preachers should demonstrate the gospel, not just talk about it; it must be about works, saving, healing and delivering – not just words.

15 As Christians, we have Scripture, what Jesus taught, a fistful of apostle's letters and two thousand years of studying behind us, yet inconsistencies still exist in our opinions.

2   The Gospel is a message to the poor, about love, hope, salvation and the eternal life given by God through Jesus Christ.

3   Repentance unto God, from sin and from a sinful way of living, is essential to receive these.

4   But who, offended at the Door, can enter His sanctuary?

5   Who, refusing the bath deserves His clean robe?

6   And who, refusing the Guide can find the Way?

7   Forcing a man to keep God's laws only makes him a hypocrite.

8   Sinners obeying God's laws think it is other people who should repent.

9   Individuals are free to walk their way; God respects their freewill, and so should we. But the individual should consider where his freewill is taking him.

10 The Gospel is an invitation, a plea for those starving to attend a banquet.

11 But those desiring *other* food will not come, no matter how attractive the tablecloth, how loud the music, or how many laws we make and enforce.

12 God is in the business of opening blind eyes, unstopping deaf ears and declaring truth, not in causing blindness, deafness and deception.

13 God is good, and takes great delight in teaching His children what is good. He has no pleasure in ignorance; therefore, falling short in this area must be due to deception, distractions or from our choice.

14 Father God expects all His children to grow up, but most of His children think they already are grown up.

15 The reason why the world has so many different religions, and why Christianity itself has so many conflicting opinions of what constitutes the way, what is the truth, and how we receive eternal life, is due entirely to self-appointed leaders.

16 Man's inability to perceive the way of righteousness, coupled with the imaginations of his own heart, makes his views and abilities to lead, far too hazardous.

17 It is an eternal law that submission to an authority transfers the traits of that authority to its subordinates.

18 Righteousness passes from Jesus to His followers through their obedience to Him. And wickedness is passed on from the instigator to the perpetrator in the same way.

19 Those disobedient to the Holy Spirit shed His covering; this places them outside of the Church, outside of Christ and outside of His kingdom.

20 Move from under the robe of the Messiah and you move outside of His covenant; both Jew and Christian need to understand this.

16 No Commandment relates to what we believe, only to how we behaviour. Our behaviour reveals what we truly believe.

2 If we walk the same road as Jesus, then we will encounter the same opposition.

3 Beware: for this means as well as facing the same temptations, we will also bump into devoutly religious

people professing to walk the same path, and worship the same God.

4 I find it amazing that the main opposition against Jesus and all the prophets came from among God's people; from dedicated men who revered Scripture, prayed in the temple, and enthusiastically sang the Psalms, while professing to know and worship God in heaven.

5 Such people, claiming to be walking His way and convinced they were right, crucified Jesus, stoned the prophets and through the Dark Ages burnt innocent people alive, tied to stakes.

6 Rather than being instructed by the Law, Jesus received tuition from His Father.

7 His Father God taught Jesus about the Law, rather than the Law teaching Him about His Father; Jesus does the same for His disciples.

8 Righteousness is a condition, not just a response.

9 Preachers, reading of Peter stepping out of his boat to walk on the water, try to persuade us to confidently step out of ours.

10 The same preachers usually overlook the fact that Peter stepped out of his boat *twice*.

11 The first time Peter walked on the water, Jesus stood in front of him, saying, *"Come!"*

12 The second time, Peter, now fearless and full of confidence, sure this time that he would not sink, put on his coat before jumping over the side.

13 Although Jesus was again before him, this time Peter had to swim for it.

14 Stepping out as Jesus beckoned him to come, was obedience, but stepping out before Jesus beckoned, was presumption.

15 Being presumptuous means always having to swim for it.

16 We arrive at unity with God, via an invitation and a command; the commandment is, *"You be holy for I Am holy"*.

17 Proof that the gospel is true, should accompany the words.

18 The poor, sick and dying need more than words, more than testimonies, they need help.

19 Each preacher should deliver more than just words; they should present Jesus, and offer life, health, freedom and peace in His name.

20 Proof that the Spirit of Christ is upon a man, is that man proclaiming the same message and doing the same works as Jesus did.

17 While with His disciples at their last meal together, Jesus said, *"Do this in remembrance of Me."* When we do, how do we remember Him?

2 It is very difficult relating to Jesus as our Healer if we are sick, or as our Deliverer if still bound.

3 Experience, not imagination, provides genuine memories; therefore, in reality, we can remember Jesus, even while breaking bread, only according to our experiences with Him.

4 If I step off a temple pinnacle while trusting God will catch me, would I be tempting Him?

5 And if I throw my medication in the bin, while trusting God will heal me, would I be tempting Him?

6 With inferior and deteriorating leadership comes an inferior, deteriorating nation.

7 Blind, unrighteous leaders create increasing legislation, and problems with it, mostly due to their dismantling and tampering with what already existed, while promising something better.

8 What blind leaders *see* is never reality, and improvements by unrighteous people, never are.

9 Fewer laws provide freedom not more.

10 Bowing our knee in pretence to our idol, while acknowledging the one true God in our mind does not work quite as we expect, for the hypocrisy is not towards the idol but towards God.

11 In the presence of an idol turn your back to it; it won't know you've done that but onlookers will.

12 If God gives you a mission then go alone, do not involve bystanders. While companionship is good, help to do what God has told *you* to do, is not.

13 Just like moths attracted to light, enthusiastic, religious bystanders will start arriving, encircle any revival flame and mingle with the crowd.

14 The genuine will be no problem, but like the Pharisees, many will come questioningly to check it out.

15 Others will come looking for signs, and still others, excited, selfish and thinking their time of fame has arrived, will seek to assist, hoping to take over.

16 At the first sign of revival, bystanders will begin to appear. Believing they have the truth, they will arrive to check revival truth against theirs.

17 Remember who the Gospel is for because jobs will arise, labelled *essential*, as will people labelled *important*, along with those clutching unsolvable problems seeking only *attention*.

18 Bystanders can occupy our time, divert our attention or simply smother us.

19 Given half a chance, bystanders will close in, overwhelm the poor and insulate them from the Good News.

20 Bystanders also have the ability, through their desires and ideas, to stress their agendas, and with polite invitations and advice, control people.

18 By laying hands upon the sick and praying for them, are we expecting more from prayer than was intended?

2 The difference between *praying* for people and *ministering* to them is probably greater than most Christians realise.

3 Yes, *faith* is necessary to *receive* a miracle, but *authority* is necessary to *provide* one.

4 Even with faith, without authority from Jesus, miracles are difficult to obtain.

5 Without His authority, a miracle will require mountains of faith.

6 Until we find the fountain, we can neither drink from it nor show others the way to it. Once found we can drink from it and send or bring others who are thirsty, so that they too may drink.

7 If we are sick, how can we expect others to believe that we have found the Healer, or the Deliverer if still bound?

8 While suffering ourselves, it is no use speaking to others of remedies.

9 One of the greatest obstacles to getting to know God is choosing for one's self a spiritual leader; other than the Holy Spirit that is!

10 All second-hand relationships are suspect, especially one with Jesus.

11 Unless we demonstrate our love, it is ineffective; thoughts and words alone are insufficient.

12 Because love is an emotion, true love shows in the way we behave; emotions are difficult to hide, they trigger action.

13 So, how do Christians, display their love towards God? It requires more than thoughts or hymns and verbal

applause because true love insists on revealing itself through behaviour.

14 The only way to show we love God is by giving Him the right to influence our lives.

15 By loving lifeless objects, we give the devil a handle by which to control us.

16 In effect, and due to the way they manipulate their lovers, idols are devils.

17 We speak well of love, but love has a notorious reputation.

18 We must not let a world full of sin, abuse, and blasphemy dictate to us what is right and wrong. Otherwise, we could all become united, and while smiling at each other, make our way, arm-in-arm to hell.

19 Hell will be packed full to the brim with souls, entirely due to love, due to the things they *loved* to think about, *loved* to talk about and *loved* to do.

20 Love itself is not righteous! True love, loves righteousness!

19 According to a Good Source of information, there are those busy in the household of the Nobleman who will not have Him reign over them.

2 With instruments, man can observe the smallest of particles, as well as the enormity of the cosmos, but he has no ability or instrument to help him see the truth in front of his eyes.

3 I have learnt from experience, no one walks with God while having dirty feet, nor works for Him with dirty hands.

4 Anyone with one eye on the pleasures of this life cannot see or experience the pleasures of the next; in this condition, if we call ourselves Christian, then we

deceive ourselves; taking His name in vain, we break the Third Commandment.

5 God does not bless sinners in the hope that they will then repent.

6 Retaliation and punishment oppose mercy! Punishment may seem warranted but mercy is greater.

7 A belief in punishment as being right provides an excuse to condemn the offender, and even torture and kill him, instead of forgiving him.

8 Jesus said, *"True worshipers will worship the Father in spirit and truth."* True worship comes from a clean, sincere heart, and only occasionally via words.

9 Many of those high priests, scribes, and Pharisees that pressured Pilate into crucifying Jesus, would have sung the Psalms to God just as enthusiastically as any worship group today.

10 Words alone can be deceptive; words accompanied by apparent worship even more so.

11 Public worship and public prayer have become, and maybe always have been, excellent opportunities to practice hypocrisy.

12 Genuine worship is true love; praise and worship before others is not necessarily genuine or true love.

13 While declaring the name of God Most High, as being theirs, Israel filled its temple and the Most Holy Place with idols.

14 Christians are likely to do the same because His sanctuary is the heart of His people.

15 Only disciples of Jesus grow up in His image, and His likeness.

16 Righteous Noah could have responded to the warning God gave him, in two ways. He could have believed it and built a boat.

17 Noah could still have believed the warning but *refused* to build the boat. If this had been his choice, the

outcome would *not* have been as obvious as one would think.

18 In times of judgement, God will not permit the righteous to suffer alongside the wicked.

19 If Noah had loved sinners sufficiently to refuse to build the boat, then God would have willingly intervened, and in protecting Noah, protected many others.

20 God often looks for a man to stand in the gap, and this was the response He was hoping would come from Noah.

20 It is much easier to find God in a wilderness than in a Jerusalem.

2 Busy people will place Jesus some way down their priority list, but in a wilderness, things are very different.

3 Wilderness places have few occupants, few alternative views, and few distractions.

4 Such places as prisons, hospitals and monasteries may serve as a wilderness, but a place among friends rarely so; we are too eager to follow and to please them.

5 In a Jerusalem, crowds, friends, family, jobs, hobbies and rituals all attract our attention.

6 Nice, attractive, friendly people distract us from Him. We want to be with them, and make some effort to make sure we are.

7 "Disagreeable people trouble us; generally, they drive us to God, if only for forgiveness."

8 It is much easier to walk with Jesus alone than in a crowd.

9 This is a narrow road; even a crowd has to walk in single file when following Jesus.

10 The interests and suggestions of individuals in any group will rarely all lie in the same direction, and we naturally take the path of least resistance.

11 Beware, religious people will speak deceptively of unity, but just the act of walking with Jesus, separates. And beware; when people speak of unity it usually means on their terms.

12 Do not be deceived; Jesus did not come to unite men, but to divide them. Following Jesus will separate you from almost everyone and everything else; false shepherds will disagree with this.

13 Heaven's crowns, authorities and rewards are only for those who overcome this world.

14 We will never overcome this world by following others and indulging ourselves in it.

15 It is necessary to reject all that the world offers to us; our desires must be for heaven and it's King.

16 Hoping to make it into heaven, only through a belief in Jesus Christ, is insecure, especially while desiring the pleasures of this world.

17 Who, while enjoying its benefits, would willingly leave one kingdom for another?

18 A desire for help or a cry for freedom must precede any rescue; otherwise, a rescue becomes an abduction; God is not into kidnapping souls.

19 Belief alone is insufficient to qualify for heaven. As the apostle James reminds us, even devils believe, and it scares the pants off of them.

20 All the children of God, just by being His children, deserve His care.

21 Again – we are what we eat! It is impossible to grow without food. All the children of Adam must eat to live.

2 To mature and live eternally, all the children of God should eat His bread; as their Father, it is His job to provide it, and our responsibility to seek, gather and consume it.

3 The 'Bread of God' is truth; His truth is food for life. His bread will teach us righteousness.

4 Jesus stressed the importance of His bread and our need for it.

5 Truth provides heavenly growth, but one must consume and digest it to benefit from it.

6 Both naturally and spiritually, it is impossible to mature *and* remain ignorant.

7 Facts are not truth; no one gets to heaven by knowing 2+2=4. Facts relate to this world, truth is food for the next.

8 There are no shortcuts to uncovering truth; it is an obscure and time-consuming task.

9 Seekers of truth have seriously dedicated adversaries.

10 Gathering knowledge and learning of wisdom is costly; all seekers of truth recognise the value of both.

11 This realization will prompt them, as far as is practical, to record what they have learnt.

12 Unless recorded, truth exists only briefly before it is lost again.

13 To regain what has been lost requires the same seeking and discovering procedure to start all over again, which is one of the reasons why Scripture is so valuable.

14 Nothing and no one is born already mature.

15 The acquisition of truth is not a pastime, it is life, and the road to maturity; maturing is the process of growing up to know God.

16 Truth is far more precious, and far more difficult to find than we generally appreciate.

17 The glorified Jesus spoke of His truth as being *"gold refined in the fire"*; this is not free, it is very expensive.

18 To buy His truth will cost us in our time; our time is our life!

19 Neither children nor adults, *accept* the truth from those whom they do not respect. Those who do not respect God cannot receive truth.

20 People do not hunger for His bread if they are satisfied with bread received from elsewhere.

22 This world is full of covetous people wanting what belongs to others.

2 Some take it violently, some by stealth, and some by begging.

3 Expecting God to provide whatever we ask is presumptuous and childish, unless that is, God has already told us that He will provide whatever we ask, for then one may confidently expect it. But Jesus said, *"First, seek the kingdom of God and then all these things will be added to you."*

4 Religious people compare Jesus Christ to other standards. Disciples of Jesus compare all other standards to Him.

5 Do we compare Jesus to the Laws of Moses or do we compare them to Him?

6 His command to *"Go..."* also came with His command to *"Wait..."* The reason for the delay was that they had to wait for Him to accompany them.

7   Unless He goes with you, how will people know He has sent you? Your affirmation would be insufficient.

8   Things are as sad as they are today because the Christian sits at the feet of other tutors, instead of in private before Jesus.

9   Receiving tuition from men, means they prepare us to their standard, rather than the Holy Spirit preparing us to His.

10 Therefore, we may be suitable to carry their word, but unsuitable to bear the word of God.

11 Those who have given their heart to Jesus Christ, beware; *entertainment* quickly retrieves it!

12 Entertainment can unite sinners and saints in the thrill of breaking all Ten Commandments.

13 What we enjoy reading and watching reveals as much, if not more, about the condition of our heart than what we say and do.

14 We are what we eat, and what entertains us feeds our soul.

15 Armageddon may already be upon us, but the weapons of war being used may not be what we were expecting.

16 The End Time battle is against the soul and not so much against the body.

17 Distractions, rather than threats, are far more powerful at polluting and diverting a saint.

18 Entertainment is a time-consuming, life-changing beautiful beast that human nature finds fascinating.

19 Love is not an easy thing to prove, words and deeds alone are insufficient.

20 Knowledge and wisdom produce spiritual growth, age not necessarily so.

23 If God were to be a control freak, then thundering from the sky, He would speak on every aspect of our lives, and everyone would obey Him instantly.

2 With such scary, heavenly intrusions, the entire world, would tremble, expecting wrath for disobedience, and hasten to obey the thunderous, demanding voice.

3 And if outright obedience to the King were to be a valid ticket into His kingdom, the entire world would then march into it rejoicing.

4 However, when it discovers He is not the terrible, strict, wrathful, vengeful, death-dealing, control freak they thought He was, but instead, meek and lowly in heart, trouble would ensue.

5 There would be a momentary stunned silence, before the entire world, now cluttering heaven, would breathe a big sigh of relief.

6 The world would immediately abandon its fear of God, and as it did so, all chaos would break loose; arguments and fighting would quickly permeate heaven.

7 Out of either fear or else for a reward, human nature can willingly obey anyone. However, fear and rewards change decisions, they do not change hearts.

8 Should the reason for fearing God disappear then so would obedience.

9 Once in possession of any reward, then love and loyalty would be on offer to anyone.

10 Seekers of rewards love the rewards, not the One offering them; they make themselves available to the highest bidder.

11 However, God has a way to test people; a way to prove their heart and justify their reward, and He must do this before they either see or hear Him.

12 Obedience towards God is good, but it must stem, not from fear or for any reward, but out of love for Him; to distinguish the difference, He must work in silence, unobserved.

13 Human nature is deceptive, and can mimic righteousness, servitude and love, and thereby fool onlookers.

14 And our human nature deceives its owner far more effectively than it does other people.

15 We can all behave ourselves before those we want to impress.

16 But before long, and at choice times, our mask slips, and our carnal nature reveals itself; the enemy is delighted when this happens, especially when it is before others.

17 If he feels compelled to justify his actions, the thief will provide excuses.

18 One common excuse is "It's not for me, it's for someone else!"

19 Willingly giving to thieves, whatever they stole, erases the sin, but demanding retribution adds another.

20 God dwells in the secret place, He listens to those who meet Him there.

24

As well as being a blessing, prayerful revision often brings fresh revelation.

2 A blind leader is bad, but not as bad as a perverted leader who can see where he is going and is determined to get there.

3 A sinner wants to do what is right but falls short.

4 A wicked person wants to do what is wrong and is determined to do it.

5 The former may repent and turn to the Saviour, but the latter, rarely, if ever!

6   Under the tuition of the Holy Spirit, parables become our friends, for they contain examples of truth and righteousness.

7   But parables also hide the truth, and without our Tutor, they have the potential to deceive us.

8   Canaan, and its acquisition, form many wonderful and beneficial parables, but it hides truth very efficiently; it still deceives vast numbers.

9   As the Israelites crossed over the Jordan to take Canaan, they gained many things, most, if not all, through violence.

10 We tread so carefully among Christians and unbelievers so as not to offend, and we often compromise our beliefs in doing so; Jesus did no such thing.

11 People accepted Him and His teachings or they did not. We have no record of Him apologising to His Father for offending anyone

12 Scripture records many instances where the judgement of wicked men involves them meeting their demise, and in nearly all cases it does so without regret.

13 It seems it is right that wicked people get what they deserve; if they do not turn from their wickedness then it is right that they keep it, and the judgement that follows.

14 In Scripture, righteous men seem to have no compassion for and lose no sleep over the loss of a wicked soul.

15 Amazingly, Scripture is full of righteous people praying for their destruction.

16 There are two incompatible seeds, each with a particular lifestyle, fruit and destiny.

17 The ability to give and create is real power, but man attributes power as being the ability to take and destroy.

18 Therefore, should God ever point the finger accusingly at the enemy, as the cause of all the pain, bloodshed and destruction, then mankind would likely turn from God and try to appease the destroyer by worshipping him.

19 However, Satan is not for appeasing, and turning away from God would be catastrophic.

20 Better that man, out of ignorance, blames God, and turns to Him for mercy and salvation, than turning and trying to pacify the slayer.

25 In character, God is unchanging, yet He loves change and variation; variation in sound, size, ability, colour, shape, motion, scent, texture and personality.

2 God is one, and yet He loves the multitude without number, and them all being different pleases Him.

3 God is over all, yet He is known as the God of Abraham, Isaac and Jacob, the God of individuals.

4 All gods and kings love to rule and dominate, but God Most High, the one true living God, is different, for He desires our friendship, and to serve and care for us.

5 God rules by love, through love, not by power through force.

6 God is all-powerful, but His strength lies in knowledge and wisdom, not in violence.

7 Before creating anything or anyone He thinks things through and prepares answers and solutions for all potential problems.

8 When compared to the majesty of God, man's greatness is insignificant, and yet our unimportance exalts Him.

9 Amazingly, in our lowliness, we increase His greatness, and by becoming meek and lowly in heart become more like Him.

10 God is everything of value in everything.
11 Love and respect for one another, does not require knowledge of the Law, or Jesus' command, but it fulfils both.
12 If we lose the joy of the Lord then it shows on our faces.
13 If we lose the joy of the Lord then it shows in what we say about Jesus, and how we say it. We may not notice this but unbelievers do, which is why they are ignoring our Good News.
14 The Star of Bethlehem was a vision to the wise, not a physical object; no one else saw it!
15 As soon as the wise men used their logic, the vision disappeared.
16 It is our assumptions that lead us astray.
17 Instead of keeping clear of Jerusalem, the wise men walked confidently into the centre of it,
18 Using logic and reasoning, vast numbers have gone to religious places seeking God in heaven, and have not found Him.
19 God dwells in the secret place; His children meet Him in private.
20 To show mercy to an offender is a righteous response, whereas a demand they be punished, is not. Only those who are offended have the right to forgive.

26 It takes opposition to reveal true character.
2　I walk, confident that the path I tread leads to heaven; however, my confidence alone is insufficient *proof* that my path *does* lead there.
3　Only my *arrival* can prove my path leads to where I say it will. Surely it would be wise for all preachers in all faiths to consider this because God will call us all to account.

4 The point is that a man's confidence alone does not qualify him to lead others.

5 How can I serve God, when all the time He is serving me?

6 How can I work for Him, when He constantly works within and for me?

7 How can I teach others about Him, when He is busy striving to teach and reveal Himself to me?

8 How can I give sight to the blind, or lead them His way, when I am just as blind as they are, and totally dependant upon Jesus and His Spirit to lead me?

9 How can I support the weak or provide legs for the lame, if I cannot myself stand up and walk His way without His help and support?

10 Can the weak provide strength, can a fool speak wisely, or the ignorant teach knowledge?

11 The heart of men is first deceptive, then desperately wicked; therefore, all the ways of men require correction.

12 Pride easily deceives man into thinking he is sufficiently strong to support others, or that he can see clearly to show others the way, as he stumbles blindly alongside them through this same wilderness.

13 The above provides ample reasons as to why God gives His Holy Spirit to each of His children.

14 We follow other men at our peril.

15 The full meaning of *praise* and *worship* is not just to *speak well* of God, but also to demonstrate His wonderful, righteous character through our lives.

16 In truth, if we are to praise and worship Him without being hypocritical, then we must live our lives in a way that demonstrates His character.

17 By what we say, and the way we live our lives, we all demonstrate the one we worship.

18 Our loving, heavenly Father is not a complicated Personality. He only seems complicated to those who only partly know Him.

19 Man finds it easier to reach for the commentary, and ask other people for their views, rather than seek God for His.

20 Only the blind and foolish, ask the blind and foolish, the way to wisdom.

27 In tribulation, some draw away from Jesus to protect themselves, while others draw closer to Jesus, for Him to protect them.

2 Rather than warfare and physical violence, the Great Tribulation spoken of in the Scriptures, may well be subtler... through entertainment and prosperity. The enemy has exhausted the previous; the latter is new.

3 Distractions entice us away from God very efficiently, while violence would probably drive us swiftly to Him.

4 Against determined saints, a distraction is far more effective than a threat.

5 Leaders offend God if they hush the children when He is trying to wake them up.

6 Those who go to the church to pray, may find the pastor and his programme standing in the way.

7 People often ask the priest, what they should only have asked of God; such, rarely get the right answer.

8 Wisdom is not illogical.

9 Seeing a fault in another does not give us the right to point it out.

10 One must be blameless, before pointing the finger, this is a truth we often overlook in our eagerness to correct others.

11 For the vast majority of Christians, all is well only while all is well.

12 At other times, all is not well, and sadly, we then suffer alongside unbelievers, join them in their queues, to ask their doctors, for their help.

13 The secret place, spoken of in Psalm 91, is a very secret place since few among us seem to have found it.

14 A glance at Scripture shows men suffering from one thing or another, even the prophets... especially the prophets!

15 Only Jesus dwelt in that secret place of abundant life and safety, and He stepped out of it willingly to suffer humiliation, affliction, pain and death to redeem us.

16 We all covet its promises, but perhaps Psalm 91 only applied to Jesus.

17 Knowledge and wisdom lead to maturity, joy comes with maturity, accompanied by a certain amount of sadness!

18 Man's knowledge and wisdom are for this life – to help him grow up; where we spend eternity depends entirely on what we grow up to become.

19 God can richly bless one man, without the man standing next to him knowing anything about it.

20 As well as in words, wisdom also manifests itself through behaviour.

28 God leads His people, not visibly, or verbally, nor by His finger writing on the wall.

2 His leadership is via tuition, rarely by vocal commands.

3 Voices, words, dreams and signs can come from anywhere and usually do; learn of Him, and His ways, and walk with Him in them.

4 Don't wait for directions, learn of Him and follow His example.

5   While rejoicing in Jesus, our *not going* does not disappoint Him, and our deciding to *go* does not guarantee a blessing on the way.

6   The important thing is that wherever we are, and whatever we are doing, we nurture and maintain a close relationship with Jesus.

7   This pleases God far more than which church, or series of meetings we attend, or what part we play in them.

8   The place where God wants us to be, all the time, is in a close relationship with His Son.

9   Being away from Jesus and distanced from Christian friends, we become vulnerable to the enemy.

10 The enemy, knowing our weaknesses, strives to cancel Christian meetings whenever and wherever he can.

11 The enemy also knows about successful warfare tactics; he too divides to conquer.

12 Having separated the lukewarm Christian from Jesus, the enemy then sets out to distance him or her from their caring brothers and sisters.

13 Cancelled meetings serve to keep Christians apart from week to week, very effectively.

14 Away from the safety provided by Jesus, and away from the relative safety provided by other believers, struggling Christians fall away.

15 In fellowships that cancel meetings frequently, often at a whim, the serpent is winning the battle;

16 By cancelling meetings, leaders stifle growth among their followers, and closing meetings gives the serpent the advantage.

17 There are no guaranteed tickets to heaven.

18 Children of God must be more determined to follow Jesus than the enemy is to stop them.

19 To ensure we arrive in the Promised Land, we must follow Jesus Christ with some determination, all the way.
20 All the heavenly rewards promised by Jesus are only for those who arrive there, but to arrive there, means overcoming all obstacles in our way.

29 Both spiritually and naturally, growth removes silliness and frivolity from one's life.
2 Silliness, among children, is not foolishness, merely natural. Silliness among adults *is* foolish because they should know better.
3 Ignorance is to be expected among children; it makes them vulnerable. There is no excuse for ignorance among adults, it is shameful, and it leaves them vulnerable too.
4 A child is more likely to observe and heed the fool, acting silly, than the wise acting wisely.
5 Should one educate the child belonging to another, without his or her parental permission?
6 Should one educate children of God, without His permission?
7 When a child's authority equals that of its mother, and a wife's that of her husband's, then anarchy reigns, restoration is only possible through either meekness or violence, and violence is unrighteous!
8 As divided houses multiply, the nation disintegrates.
9 Life may be boring, busy or dangerous but it is not funny; for most people, life is a very serious issue.
10 People turn from their sinful way of living to God during times of danger, when distressed, never in moments of hilarity, entertainment and pleasure. To experience pleasure where we are, will mean staying there.

11 There is no path to maturity without discarding silliness and toys; silliness and toys keep us childlike, toys serve as idols.

12 There is no path to maturity without experiencing and integrating the serious side of life.

13 Reproduction applies spiritually as well as naturally.

14 Reproduction is a combination of seed, birth, provisions, instruction and examples; it's the same for the kingdom of heaven.

15 But the Gospel Seed sown by Jesus is not necessarily the same gospel seed sown by people today.

16 Nevertheless, the seeds that are sown by people today, still produce disciples – usually theirs.

17 Spiritual seed, like the natural seed, bears a genetic code of its parentage; of what and who we are.

18 Therefore, traits of Jesus, mixed with traits of man, will combine to give gospel seed containing some resemblance to Jesus but with human flaws.

19 How serious those flaws are could mean sowing wheat destined for heaven or sowing tares destined for burning.

20 We do reproduce 'after our own kind' but if we are a mixture of goodness and badness, truth and lies, then our seed will reflect that.

30 The apostle Paul taught that chatterboxes should keep quiet in meetings. This view is quite agreeable, and one only likely to offend chatterboxes. However, leaders also use this view to silence everyone else.

2 The Bible teaches that a man should yield his will to Jesus Christ, which is opposed only by rebellious men.

3 The Bible teaches that the wife should yield to her husband, which is opposed only by rebellious wives.

4 God commands all children to honour their parents, which is also opposed only by rebellious children.

5 Rebels are in danger of failing to enter heaven's gates.

6 It isn't far off to say that God has only one rule, which is that we follow Jesus and heed His word.

7 The message that John the Baptiser preached in the wilderness was so good that it turned people from their existing way of living to seek God.

8 It influenced them sufficiently for them to deplore whatever God disapproved of, and to wash themselves clean from all of it.

9 Whatever it was that John's message contained, the people certainly thought it Good News; to the religious leaders however, it was abominable. What was it that John preached to offend those leaders?

10 People, who preach the same Good News as Jesus, can expect the same reception from the poor, and the same reception, as He did, from religious leaders.

11 Like the Pharisee, could we be so zealous for the Scriptures that, by not knowing God, we could oppose His Son?

12 The priests were comparing Jesus of Nazareth with their Scriptures, instead of comparing their Scriptures with Jesus of Nazareth.

13 Valuing Scripture, as being the Word of God, has an appearance of being wise, but this is exactly what the hypocritical scribes and Pharisees did.

14 One does not have to know God to speak well about Him; the nations of Israel and Judah did this right up to their destruction.

15 Likewise, one does not have to know Jesus Christ to speak well about Him, Christianity has done this throughout its atrocious history and will do until the end.

16 The danger, which nations fail to see, is that without a relationship with Jesus, we can mention His name, and even speak well about Him, and yet, at the same time, oppose Him.

17 If, while living unrighteous lives and cherishing our idols, we speak well of God, God does not speak well of us.

18 All jobs have strings attached to them.

19 But a *gift* with strings attached is a contract.

20 Pubs are open every day, for their managers to welcome people, not so churches.

31 Leadership is lordship; think about that!

2 The leader we follow determines the God we follow.

3 People, determined to lead others, eventually meet other likeminded souls determined to lead them, when this occurs there is always friction, and someone must either yield or leave.

4 Leadership and its failings have plagued mankind from the beginning.

5 Even the fight between Cain and Abel could quite easily have been due to leadership.

6 Cain, being the elder, but unrighteous, may have expected righteous Abel to knuckle under and follow his example.

7 One striving to dominate another is the cause of all dissension; whereas respecting our neighbour, erases all contention.

8 Jesus explained to His disciples, the greatest among them would not be the loudest, the most handsome nor the strongest, but the meekest of all. The crowns are not for works but for behaviour.

9 To follow Jesus is not to seek leadership; to seek leadership is to follow the chief priests and Pharisees.

10 Christ is and will always be the King because He is not dependant upon His people saving, providing and caring for Him; instead, He saves, provides and cares for them.

11 Our level of love for Jesus will determine our level of faithfulness to Him.

12 Our level of love for Jesus will determine how far along the road we will walk with Him.

13 There are no rules or threats in the kingdom of God.

14 If He had to threaten men to get them into His kingdom, then He would have to threaten them to keep them there.

15 People enter the kingdom of God through abandoning their domain and surrendering to His.

16 The Promised Land is not a prison; it has no walls or boundaries;

17 People who are permitted to enter it dwell there voluntarily.

18 Most of us know right from wrong, but if we want one, an excuse is easy to find. An excuse is common among lawbreakers.

19 Depending on how we read Scripture, it can be a real pleasure, mediocre or a complete waste of time.

20 The Bible is not our God nor our Saviour, so we shouldn't let it speak to us as though it is.

32 When both national and religious leaders go awry, then prophets from God start turning up, not to lead and comfort His people, but to warn them to repent, or else!

2 In truth, the Christian only worships God, truthfully and in spirit, as he or she walks out of church, with Jesus, to spend the rest of their week with Him.

3 Walking in the way God planned for us is true worship.

4 Men who serve, rather than manage, and men who give wisely, rather than take foolishly, are closer to heaven than the rest of us.

5 Only a man with no relationship with God needs to seek a prophet. Only a man with a poor relationship with Jesus needs a shepherd and tutor.

6 Do not be deceived; today, there are very few prophets of God, but countless prophets of Baal, and it has always been so.

7 Beware of the one who approaches with a word from God; we are supposed to judge angels.

8 Also, beware of the one summing up what you have shared, lest he vomit all over it.

9 Talkative bystanders cannot resist a nudge from the enemy to comment on truth, expound upon it and give their views of it.

10 Through comment and opinion, the enemy uses talkative people to smother and pollute the truth.

11 God cringes when one of His children prosecutes another.

12 To prosecute your neighbour is to be unforgiving and desire recompense; neither are heavenly traits.

13 When His children complain, God takes it personally.

14 God is our guide, our provider and our protector; therefore, to grumble and complain about life is to show disrespect towards Him. Grumblers and complainers are unlikely to qualify for entrance into His kingdom.

15 God takes what we say to and about other people, as though we are saying it to and about Him. What we say about other people and what we do to them shows God what kind of people we are.

16 Praising God while criticizing your neighbour is hypocrisy.

17 The Pharisees, presuming spiritual knowledge, spiritual ability, and the authority of God, could produce only imaginary fruit – religious converts. It is our presumptions that lead us astray.

18 Jacob said, *"...I have seen God face-to-face and my life is preserved,"*

19 Paraphrased, Jacob said, 'I have met God and my life has been extended' or put another way, Jacob said, 'I have met with God and He has given me eternal life;' and I think this much clearer. Is this not the Gospel?

20 God does not wrestle with a man except to turn him around and give him life; that involves a very real, and sometimes lengthy struggle.

33 When asked, we all have a legitimate right, at any time, to say "no!" It can be careful or careless to say "no!" but it is not being selfish, selfishness is using people for one's own benefit.

2 God never *uses* people!

3 Jesus did not parade those whom He healed and delivered before the crowds to advertise His ministry.

4 He was content to see those whom He loved delivered from their torment.

5 Some preachers today, *use* people at every opportunity, they say, it is to build faith and glorify God, but it is to draw people's attention to themselves and their ministry.

6 For sure, you cannot silence a man truly blessed of God; give him space and he will testify convincingly.

7 Could it be that signs and wonders follow the gospel, and not necessarily the preacher?

8 Preparation provides the ability, ability leads to employment, employment warrants authority, and authority produces fruit.

9 Salvation is a twofold event that takes time, redemption through the blood of Jesus Christ, and a process of purification by the Holy Spirit.

10 Through the prophet, the Spirit said, *"The heart of man is deceitful above all things, and desperately wicked, who can know it?"* So, how can it possibly be safe for one man to lead or teach another?

11 God is not a thief, so He cannot just take sin away, or confiscate our idols without our permission; yet somehow, carefully and respectfully, He has to remove whatever hinders us from entering His kingdom.

12 Perhaps He has no other option than to withdraw a little distance from us, and lead us into a wilderness. Eventually, at some point, like the prodigal son, we come to our senses, repent, and turn back to Him.

13 I struggle to imagine what else *pruning* could mean, for this procedure does seem to have removed detritus and stimulated spiritual growth in me.

14 For sure, we could not backslide while in His presence; therefore, backsliding can only occur if we distance ourselves from Him.

15 Only as we see and reject the distraction, can we turn back to God, and only then will He fellowship with us again.

16 God watches over His children all the time; He can see the essential things that we must discard from our lives, and He knows how to reveal them to us.

17 Without repentance from sin, it is impossible to maintain a relationship with God.

18 This wilderness was never meant to be a place of comfort, leisure and pleasure.

19 To coast through life, in comfort and blessings, would not serve to highlight the very things within us that are preventing us from entering His Promised Land.

20 Do we love the onions, garlic and meat of Egypt or the scrumptious delicacies that the world provides through entertainment, more than the Manna God provides?

34 Like iron to a magnet, perversions on the inside are attracted to perversions on the outside; only the right decision will keep them apart.

2 If the two meet up, power is then required to separate them; God is not a thief, He will not take away what we cling to.

3 Human nature within us seeks the food on which it feeds, and if we cannot crucify it outright then we must starve it to death.

4 Do not mistake a desire to teach, lead and pastor others, as a desire to serve Jesus.

5 Sometimes we fail to show due respect towards Jesus.

6 Instead of treating Him as our Lord and Master, occasionally we treat Him like a very rich uncle.

7 We visit Him periodically, usually when we want something, and we flatter Him profusely, before getting around to why we came. We do this, hoping we have flannelled Him enough to stir His generosity and open His wallet.

8 After many words, many smiles and waving at Him in worship, we become confident that we have softened His heart sufficiently and often enough, for us to benefit in His will.

9 Jesus gives men authority over sin, sickness and the devil, never over people.

10 Jesus, rather than describing a management structure to His disciples, speaks of His apostles as being servants and brethren.

11 To the religious leaders opposing Him, Jesus promised to send them *"prophets, wise men and scribes"* and some of them they would persecute and kill.

12 Had the apostle Paul seen or heard this remark, then I am sure he would have also included *wise men* and *scribes* somewhere on his lists of church ministries.

13 Those who come to know God will discover He is meek and lowly in heart. The characteristics of a meek and lowly heart, involve Him loving and caring for all He creates, which prevents Him from killing and destroying any of it.

14 Therefore, His rejection of violence, and His refusal to destroy, is His weakness.

15 To maintain His meek and lowly character, God must conquer and be forever victorious without ever getting angry or becoming violent.

16 God does not create in haste, but thinks things through first; then, forewarned, He has a victorious solution for every foreseen problem and every foreseen word or deed of any potential enemy.

17 For this reason, the enemies of God cannot outsmart or surprise Him, for He was already aware of their intentions from the start.

18 Therefore, God's strength is His foreknowledge, and His wisdom in applying it.

19 God is not, in any way, like men, His foolishness and His weakness surpasses all man's wisdom and man's strength.

20 While triumphing over all His enemies, He maintains intact, His meek and lowly heart – not through violence, but by His knowledge and wisdom.

35 God instructed us to be holy because He is holy. Holiness, as well as meaning separated from the world unto God, also means mature in righteousness.

2 One cannot be holy without righteous maturity; we must cut sin off – all round.

3 And the phrase, *"seeing God,"* means to *"understand Him."* Unless we mature in righteousness we will never understand God.

4 In 'The Revelation of Jesus Christ' it is sometimes assumed that the messengers of the seven churches were angelic beings.

5 But heavenly beings do not need warnings, rebukes or encouragement sent in a letter via John.

6 Jesus was speaking to the leadership of each of those seven churches.

7 Jesus acknowledges them as leaders because His people in those churches accepted them as their leaders.

8 In this case, notice how out of respect, Jesus is speaking to the leaders, not to the people.

9 And notice also how His people had already turned from following Jesus, to follow other men.

10 Wayward leaders of God's people are not unusual; historically, Israel was plagued with them, as is Christianity.

11 Church meetings, occurring behind closed doors that exclude the least of His brethren, also exclude Jesus.

12 Jesus is not in the midst to counsel where His lesser brothers are excluded.

13 Church meetings, occurring behind closed doors that exclude brethren, are devilish!

14 This applies to leader's meetings, leader's training days, leaders conferences and all such *select* religious events.

15 Tuition, planning and decisions in closed meetings, occur without any input from the Holy Spirit. But the enemy is free to contribute whatever he can.

16 Try not to speak words without understanding. For the word 'grace' read 'help' and for the word 'faith' read 'confidence'.

17 According to Jesus, eternal life is *'knowing* God', not working for Him.

18 The apostle James spoke well of *works*, but maybe we misunderstand, he probably meant *behaviour*; bad people can do good works!

19 Faith in Jesus, while lacking good behaviour, is false, as is good behaviour that excludes Jesus!

20 But through faith in Jesus, the Holy Spirit will teach us what is good and what is bad behaviour.

36 Assuming importance, and taking the best seat, reveals the betrayer.

2 Oppose the world, and it will rise against you.

3 Befriend the world, and it will welcome you as a hypocritical Christian.

4 But while ever we remain silent and do not oppose the ways of the world, then the world takes it that we approve of its ways and tolerates us; thus we become the tail and not the head.

5 If the Scriptures were truly the Word of God, then it would be possible to enter heaven without ever developing a relationship with God.

6 We could talk to the book, let it talk to us, and follow the advice it gives to us.

7 Beware; do not treat the instruction book as the Instructor, or the guidebook as the Guide.

8 When it suits him and his purpose, the enemy can quote Scripture profoundly.

9   Placing our children under the tuition of other people allows them to write their beliefs on their hearts, and implant their behaviour into their lives.

10 Everything was very good in the beginning, even the Tree of the Knowledge of Good and Evil!

11 The point God stressed to Adam was that it was not good to eat from that tree; it was not for consumption.

12 God had already told them what to eat, but Adam ate something God did not provide to be eaten; something that was sinful to eat.

13 The devil was a murderer from the beginning! Prompted by the serpent, Eve killed, and they both ate of its flesh!

14 Opposition occurs as much from refusing to submit to authority, as it does from differences in belief.

15 People can believe whatever they like – providing they are willing to bow the knee and obey the leader.

16 Between holding differing views and bowing the knee, bowing the knee wins every time.

17 Actions speak louder than words and far louder than thoughts.

18 Praying to God while submitting to another authority is to dishonour Him and honour the other authority; but He is very forgiving.

19 We cannot praise God with our words and bow the knee to those who oppose Him.

20 Rather than in word, worship is more in behaviour.

37 Those appearing to have abundance, now, may well have considerably less, later.

2   And those appearing to have very little, now, may well prove to be very rich, later. This is because we look at the tent, rather than the one dwelling within it.

3   There can be no hypocrisy without a tent to hide in.

4 Death removes the tent; the resurrection will reveal each of us, as we are, what we will have grown to become.

5 It seems that to become a disciple of Jesus, they had to forsake all else, and all others, to follow Him each day, every day, everywhere – and we think we are disciples!

6 The idea that *we* know, that *we* are the chosen, and that *we* are the blessed, while those in disagreement with us, are sinners, and unless they repent, are due for the wrath of God, has proved very popular for thousands of years, in all religions.

7 We misunderstand! Contrary to what we preach, God does not love the world. The world is in no condition for Him to love it.

8 Only Perfect Goodness could rule eternity.

9 For a rebellious child, a rebuke, rather than a toffee, is more appropriate

10 Momentarily, the rebuke hides the love the parent has for the child, but without the rebuke, the rebel will never truly deserve the toffee.

11 God does not work to a timetable; instead, He responds to conditions prevalent at the time.

12 True, He does know the timing of events, but it is not the time that triggers His response, but the conditions; therefore, we control the seasons!

13 A rigid timescale would prove unsuitable when dealing with independent people having the freedom to live their lives their way.

14 For meetings to survive, the one with the key to the door has to be as keen as everyone else.

15 If we do not have it, then we cannot give it to others.

16 If we are not experiencing it, then we should not share it as though we are.

17 The love Jesus had for me never faltered, even to the end; therefore, with His help, I am determined that my love for Him will never falter, even to the end.

18 We do not journey alone.

19 How can we not rejoice when the King travels with us?

20 If the King travels with you then the journey alone will be worth it.

38 *"Our God is a consuming fire!"* He purifies whatever we place on His altar.

2 Superficially, fire is a spectacle, even pleasurable, but in reality, it destroys whatever will burn, and purifies everything else that will not.

3 Fire is not enthusiasm, as is often portrayed. Fire hurts flesh; it is destructive to sin, to our carnality, to our impure nature. Many who sing, "Send the fire..." do not know what they are asking.

4 Our love for the Saviour compels we build a sacrificial altar on which to place, not our things, but ourselves. God's people were misled; originally, bringing a dead animal before the God who gave it life, was to confess you had sinned by killing it.

5 There is a murderous Cain, a covetous Jacob, a lustful David, a lying Ananias and Sapphira, and even a betraying Judas in each of us; we were all born with the same nature.

6 Communal hymn singing provides plenty of opportunities for us to promise Jesus everything in public, while secretly holding back the major portion.

7 What did the Israelites forfeit for rejecting God in favour of having a king? In fact, what does every man forfeit by choosing an alternative shepherd to Jesus Christ? The answer is simple; we forfeit experiencing the 23rd Psalm

8 God's strength lies in His foreknowledge, not in the ability to destroy; any fool can destroy, and they do, but it takes knowledge and wisdom to overpower tyranny, without being an even greater tyrant.

9 The poor have nothing, nothing to cling to; therefore, nothing to lose and everything to gain by accepting Jesus; the Good News is for these; signs and wonders fascinate the rest of us.

10 Due to the Reformation, we in the Western Nations have enjoyed the freedom of conscience.

11 We are still free to worship the God of the Bible without persecution, at any time and almost anywhere.

12 However, this privilege has produced feeble, shallow, worldly Christians.

13 Before freedom can become beneficial, there must be a genuine heartfelt desire and determination to follow Jesus.

14 The result of freedom without hunger is weak Christians who bind themselves; they worship almost secretively behind closed doors, embarrassed to speak of Jesus their King.

15 The result of having freedom of conscience, without the fear of God, means ignoring God's Law, but without God's Law, nations deteriorate.

16 If we are not careful, freedom will cause us to choose the easy, wide, and crowded road to destruction, as it did for the nation of Israel.

17 To children, all things are right! They overlook danger, disregard respect, and enjoy carelessness.

18 As children, we ignore the reality of eternity and live in the here and now.

19 To remind us of eternity, God provided the cosmos.

20 The countless stars and galaxies set in unfathomable space is His way of presenting eternity to mankind.

39 If while sat in His class I learn something new, should I then teach others? Do students teach other students, or do we all need the Tutor?

2   Jesus is Lord! He is the Shepherd! To receive His truth, people should go to Him for it; the Manna I collect is not for feeding my neighbour; he should gather his own.

3   *"But you, be not called teachers; for One is your Teacher, the Christ, you are all brethren."*

4   Unless the Holy Spirit reveals the truth to us, we will misunderstand Scripture, and likely disagree with the truth shared by a brother.

5   Misunderstanding Scripture gives it the power to crucify Jesus from our lives and destroy us.

6   It is our assumptions that lead us astray.

7   Goats and tares are visible as those who have a form of Godliness, but who have no relationship with Jesus.

8   The preacher stands to represent God and proclaim His word; therefore, he should at least have heard that word from God, and at best have Him with him when sharing it.

9   All Judea went out to be baptised by John the Baptiser, so when John identified the scribes, Pharisees and chief priests as being *"Children of the viper,"* he was only speaking of the religious Jews, not the Children of Israel.

10 John the apostle saw the same; when he refers to the Jews opposing Christ and His followers; again, he was only speaking about the religious leaders, not the Children of Israel.

11 They all thought they were Jews until Jesus appeared. Some knelt to worship Him, others stood to question Him. Both His presence and persecution sort the sheep from the goats!

12 We may all consider ourselves to be Christian; only when Jesus appears will it become obvious who is and who isn't.

13 Only in His presence do sheep and goats become obvious.

14 Do not be presumptuous about what Jesus said, or you will be confused when it does not appear. It's brief, but warnings need to be brief.

15 The hardest and most dangerous place to prepare the way of the Lord, to make His paths straight, and to smooth out the rough, is in a Jerusalem, in a church, in a religion, in any religion.

16 Traditions are cast in concrete; you waste time, effort and potentially your life, trying to remove them.

17 A lamb placed among wolves' stands little chance of surviving intact for very long. Come to think of it, the Lamb placed among the religious elite also stood little chance of surviving very long.

18 The Bible shows us that it takes evil people, and religious people, only a short time before they both slaughter the Lamb.

19 The reasons for the seasons are many, but generally, men cycle in and out of revelling in the world, and being desperate to get out of it.

20 At certain points in this cyclic behaviour, God sows and reaps His harvest.

40 Ideally, music should support the heart singing to God, not the other way round.

2 Regarding worship, rhyme is of greater importance than rhythm.

3 During worship, the soul vocalising praise to God is the most important, never the music.

4 Volume is impressive; it may excite us, but is God listening to it?

5 Above the din, maybe He's trying to hear what His people are saying!

6 Where it is abused, loud noise reveals ignorance, and a lack of respect towards God, and those within earshot. God is not deaf!

7 Sometimes, praying for people does little good; as God told Moses, they need to make an effort and keep moving forwards themselves.

8 *"Your word is a lamp to my feet and a light to my path."*

9 But how can a man walk according to God's ways, unless He first receives instruction from Him about His ways?

10 Followers are not necessarily believers.

11 One follows Jesus for what he gets out of Him, another covets His power, yet another has doubts that He is the Messiah, and another follows, but refuses to have Him rule over him.

12 Both naturally and spiritually, "We are what we eat!" therefore, men grow and mature to become like their tutors. Inevitably we will think like them, speak like them and behave like them.

13 Every tutor is unique; therefore, every student of every tutor will be unique, thus disagreement is certain.

14 Disciples of Jesus, being taught only by Him, bond together. Jesus said, *"If they will listen to Me then they will listen to you!"*

15 When Paul visited the saints in Jerusalem and met James, Peter and John, he chose to refer to them as 'pillars' of the church.

16 At that time, Paul did not call any of them by the titles on his lists, or by any we use today.

17 Protestant Churches and nations fail their subjects by not teaching their children and their converts

our history – where we came from, and how saints suffered to obtain the freedom we, and our nation, experience; therefore, we will lose it again, next time to the same enemy of our souls.

18 To distinguish the meek and repentant, from the proud and independent, God hides the truth.

19 He must do this so that we come to Him for it and so avoid being deceived; go elsewhere, and deception becomes a probability.

20 The 'Truth' is the 'Bread of Life' – the fruit of the Tree of Life. It was hidden from men, lest unsuitable people partake of that fruit, live and populate eternity.

41 *"His ways are not like our ways, and the way He thinks is not the way we think."*

2 Scripture warns man not to attribute human characteristics to God Most High.

3 Nevertheless, we still insist that occasionally He gets angry, violent and destructive, just like we do.

4 However, we are not wiped off the face of the earth, for our sin and blasphemies, precisely because He *never* gets angry, violent or destructive.

5 It is usual for one Christian to pray for another while laying hands on them.

6 But the difference between *praying* for people and *ministering* to them is probably greater than we think.

7 Prayer is communication with God; no one else needs to be there.

8 'Ministry' is not praying to God for others it is providing whatever they need.

9 Any tribulation will quickly divide the casual churchgoer from those who love Jesus.

10 Just because the Lord foretells what will happen, it does not necessarily mean He is the one bringing it to pass; think about that!

11 There is something odd about crowds; prompted or driven, a crowd tends to move as one.

12 As well as gathering to worship and celebrate, crowds also unite for war, to condemn, to stone people and to shout, *"Crucify!"*

13 People are rather like words – among a multitude, there is always sin.

14 We cannot take our lust with us into God's presence because, in His presence, lust evaporates, to leave only tears.

15 As Christians, we speak highly of God, to others.

16 As Christians, we sing of His goodness, while among others.

17 As Christians, we lavish praises upon Him, before others.

18 As Christians, many of us pray to Him, before others.

19 How well does what we sing, say and do before others, match up with what we sing, say and do out of sight of others?

20 Jesus explained to His disciples that His Father God dwells in the secret place, and listens to those who meet Him there.

42 As a new convert to Christianity, a friend explained 'tithing' to me, saying, "One-tenth of your income belongs to God; withholding it is to rob Him of His share."

2 I accepted what that Christian friend said; now I cannot release myself from this bondage without my conscience telling me I am robbing God.

3   My conscience, never silent for very long, speaks to me; I sometimes think it is the voice of God!

4   Many preachers stress handing over offerings and tithes to support their ministry. They use Scripture to encourage me to hand it over, and Scripture to condemn me should I consider refusing.

5   I testify here that at no time has God ever asked me to tithe, or even give an offering, but countless preachers have.

6   If I yield to my conscience, then it praises my obedience, but if I refuse, it condemns me, but my conscience is not my God.

7   The world is full of covetousness because a covetous little god is running it.

8   Everyone wants what belongs to his or her neighbour, and they are likely to use every means at their disposal to acquire it, both promises and threats; all children should be warned of this, including all God's children.

9   To grow up and avoid abuse, disasters and hell, children must learn when to say "no!"

10 God's children rejoice during persecution only if the cause of the problem is inside others. Internal strife removes joy.

11 Encounters with difficult people, uncover both hidden qualities and hidden problems within us.

12 Our fears, our striving, our complaining and annoyance, etc., are all signs of things wrong within us, which we should cut out and discard.

13 There is no better place to mature than in this life, for there will be no opposition, no conflict, and no troubles or trials to overcome in heaven, and only irresistible putrefaction in hell.

14 It is important to recognise that God's righteous nature does not override His righteous love, His righteous mercy or His righteous judgement of sin.

15 The fruit of the vine is a blessing only so long as it remains juice; once fermented, it has the potential to drag the king and his kingdom to its knees, the honourable to the gutter, the innocent to depravity and the saint to hell.

16 How many, idolising wine, quote as an excuse, "All things in moderation" only to find what once brought an exultant flush to their cheeks, now has them by the throat; this is true of all vices.

17 If I did not know better, I could easily jump to the *wrong* conclusion and point to this fruit as being the forbidden fruit in the Garden of Eden.

18 I can learn the truth by reading what Jesus said to others, but I could also be presumptuous and read it as though He was speaking to me.

19 So who among us is the most important, is it the pastor, the worship leader, the elder, or the cleaner? No, all such can take care of themselves!

20 Most important are our children; they need our care and attention to ensure their safe journey through life, and into the kingdom.

43 Along with the rats in the sewer, vultures in the desert and ants in the anthill, humans thrive then die.

2 Biologically, we have no guarantee that we will survive and live on into eternity; God did not design flesh and blood as eternal substances.

3 To enter and dwell in God's eternal spiritual kingdom, we must be eternal and spiritual.

4 The truth is that when we leave this world, nothing connected or belonging to it will go with us, not one atom!

5 Do not put your trust in knowledge, for we also leave this behind, and many, through illness, lose it before they go.

6 It is what we are growing up to become that counts, for that is how we will stand before God.

7 What we believe is not a guaranteed ticket to heaven, but being a friend of Jesus is.

8 This world, even with its current dangers and trials, still provides a suitable place for our spiritual conception and birth; and also, somewhere for us to prepare for eternity, somewhere for us to grow up.

9 The biggest obstacles on our life-long journey come from within us.

10 To progress along the Christian way requires that we walk, not study; it is not about head knowledge it is about growth, distance walked, which has nothing to do with how long we have been Christians.

11 No flames of holy fire will appear on our heads, or any mantle of service fall across our shoulders until the Holy Spirit is satisfied that we have learned what He intends teaching us.

12 It is better to obey God rather than risk sacrificing our sanity by struggling in our own strength.

13 As Christians, we may think that by our words and the way we live our lives, we are pointing the lost to Jesus, but often we find they are not really listening, not even looking, nor seemingly wanting to.

14 Unlike the world, the Holy Spirit teaches in small doses, putting truth in as few words as possible and in the clearest, simplest way – precept upon precept, line upon line.

15 Just like the natural variety, we must receive, consume and digest spiritual food before we can benefit from it. It must become part of us.

16 Theological Colleges, Bible Schools and even the humble Bible Study are all great contributors to the illusion that we can grow as fast as we can learn.

17 It is normal for Christians hearing of a particular truth in the first Bible Study, to show no sign of benefiting from it, by the last.

18 Beware; our spiritual ascent to heaven occurs only at the same rate as our sinful nature's descent to the grave, not how quickly we learn doctrine.

19 The youth entering class and learning the most significant and profound scientific formula comes out of a classroom only half an hour older – knowledge is not growth.

20 At the beginning of the Gospels, Jesus called men away from their father's household, to follow Him to a land that He would show them, just as God did to Abraham, and just as He does to everyone.

44 True servants of God are neither mighty men of valour, in a worldly sense, pillars of the church, in a religious sense, or someone who has authority in a legal sense.

2 God's servants are His servants and no one else's.

3 Not until the end of the Gospels does Jesus say, *"Go ye into all the world ..."* and in reality, not until after Pentecost.

4 What occupied the period between their calling and their sending was their preparation.

5 Meditation with the Holy Spirit is both revision and spiritual research.

6 Words of endearment coming from man's deceitful heart, via his fickle feelings, do not convince God of our devotion.

7 Proof of our love for God is in our obedience to Him; this is where the manna that He scatters around our camp comes in.

8 Loving submission to our Father God is important because we cannot grow up to be like Him any further, or more quickly than the love for Him in our heart permits.

9 Father God desires that all His children grow up, but it is our desire for Him that determines by how much we will grow to become like Him.

10 It is our desire for His way that determines how far we will walk along His way with Him.

11 Although survival may be sufficient to reach our destination, God desires we grow in strength and wisdom during our journey.

12 God's Laws are not just to please Him and annoy us; they are for our benefit.

13 Human nature hates laws and ignores or opposes them.

14 Teachers can only teach up to their level, so, if we place our spiritual education in the hands of other people, instead of the Saviour's, then we limit the extent to which we can grow.

15 This cycle is repetitive, and through spiritual generation after spiritual generation, an invisible ceiling prevents Christians from reaching maturity.

16 Therefore, our pastors and teachers create for us a maximum level of spiritual growth, above which we cannot rise.

17 Individuals can break free from this limitation only if they reject man's leadership and turn, seeking to follow only Jesus Christ.

18 If they do this, then they will eventually learn that only preparation provides the ability, only the ability

warrants employment and only in His employment do we have His authority to teach the nations.

19 Therefore, our full potential (maturity) is only possible if we choose Jesus for ourselves and remain faithful to Him; otherwise, by following men, we will all learn to recite the words and repeat the rituals to become far more religious than holy.

20 A *request* from a dominant character is a *command* in disguise. To prove this true, refuse the request, but be ready for a scowl, the rumours or greater pressure.

45 God does not favour those having wealth, stealth, strength, capability, social status or a persuasive tongue, above those who do not.

2 Great despair and great defeats are wonderful opportunities for great joy and great victories, providing we turn to the great God to turn things around for us and get us out of our mess.

3 Emotions and feelings have a powerful influence on our decisions; this increases our inability to distinguish right from wrong.

4 True servants of God, lead by example, not through any form of authority, supervision or management.

5 Part of growing up involves taking a tumble now and again, but we must learn from our mistakes; otherwise, we keep tumbling.

6 The lives and words of the vast majority of Christians have a negligible effect upon the hearts of the lost. No conviction, no acceptance, no objection, equals no effect.

7 We are ineffective witnesses to the resurrection of Jesus because the vast majority of so-called Christian preachers, teachers and leaders today, are all talk and no power.

8 In the church, as well as in the world, the underlying danger for students of vocal callings is self-importance.
9 Having an exaggerated image of the importance of what we think, say and do, is fatal.
10 There is ample evidence of this very effective blindfold in the politician, the teacher, and the salesman; preachers are salesmen.
11 Self-importance is a crippling disease to any potential disciple of Jesus Christ.
12 The church should minister and serve each other in, by and through fellowship.
13 In every case, daily Manna is for you and your family's consumption; God does not give it to you for other households. The instruction is for them to develop their relationship with Him by seeking and gathering their own.
14 While the desire of children to share their bread is very acceptable, a determination on their part to push it down the throats of others is not.
15 But an apparent error shared by a brother, must not be shot down too speedily, for we all have different abilities and imperfect ways of explaining precisely how we are seeing things.
16 Love and patience do not jump in, jump on, and crush the hesitant.
17 Greater errors exist among the solidly religious that are entrenched in their Christian faith, sure that they know and can see, than the young convert who, after looking to their newfound Saviour, hesitantly tries to share how he or she has glimpsed something.
18 Encourage innocence; do not smother it.
19 Truth has great depth, which could mean that the friend or the speaker we suspect as being in error, maybe a little deeper than we are, and therefore, his

or her bread a little too crusty for our young, soft palettes.

20 Thinking we know (and we all think we do) and the impulse to correct others (which we all have) are both signs of immaturity.

46 God is as good as His Word! Like Him, we are as good as our word, which of course is not very good.

2   Christ died to save us; we must be willing to die to save others.

3   Purity is a requirement of both the missionary and the mission.

4   With or without our understanding, *"such as I have, I give unto you."* is *always* the case, and never 'such as I pray, you will get'.

5   If we have nothing, then we can give nothing.

6   If you cannot provide it, then do not preach and offer it, lest you destroy confidence in Jesus.

7   Due to his blindness, a man follows his chosen shepherds, looks in the wrong direction, heeds the wrong advice, and eats from the hands of other men, stale bread.

8   The kingdom of God is not a democracy.

9   The use of a democratic process in a Christian organisation indicates, primarily, the influence of the religious spirit, and secondly that none of those involved, truly understand the basic principles of His kingdom.

10 Elections and drawing lots are how men operate, not God.

11 Those in Christ's Church have no vote in choosing His servants.

12 This means that if a Christian church insists on calling itself 'Christian', then it is by its own words

condemning all its elected staff, stewards and ordained ministers as false.

13 All titles, positions and authorities appointed by people and committees, be they pope, bishop, president, prophet, pastor, teacher, leader, etc., are all part of deceptive church structures designed by the religious spirit.

14 Such team-leaders, elbow the Holy Spirit out of their meetings and organisations, and thereby squeeze the life out of both the Christian meeting and the Christian, to leave nothing more than – business as usual.

15 A religious programme usually excludes the Holy Spirit.

16 Whereas the world promotes the competent, worships the achievers, and loves the physically beautiful, these count as nothing in heaven, for we leave them all in the grave.

17 Natural abilities do not impress God; He is looking for something far more precious and enduring – humility, not ability.

18 Rather than contribute to man's pride, God gives the incompetent, the irresponsible and even the incapable among His children, an equal opportunity to excel – providing they are prepared to walk humbly with Him and learn their lessons.

19 Those who compromise on one thing will compromise on others. True *'unity'* is based on the truth, not on compromise.

20 Compromise on truth and you will exchange Jesus as your shepherd for someone else; anyone willing to compromise on the truth is the enemy of your soul, not your brother.

47 The true sanctuary has always consisted of the hearts of God's people. Moses only saw a pattern of this, and he built the Tabernacle with its Holy Places accordingly.

2 I *never* view Jesus Christ, as being my high priest!

3 Taught that the high priest stood to minister before God for the people, we overlook how high priests and their subordinates slaughtered millions of innocent creatures.

4 They also kept the Scriptures hidden from the people, and they introduced idols into the sanctuary. The true sanctuary is the heart of God's people.

5 Likewise, through the dark ages, the Christian high priests, and their regimes slaughtered countless innocent souls. They too kept the Scriptures hidden from the people and introduced idols into the sanctuary.

6 Of all people, high priests and their subordinates have been the least holy, and most unlikely people to represent Jesus Christ.

7 Someone said, *"Behold the Lion of Judah ... and John turned and saw a Lamb, as though it had been slain..."*

8 Rather than any high priest, it is the lambs the high priest slaughtered that represented Jesus.

9 Rather than any high priest, it was Jesus who preached good news to the poor.

10 Rather than any high priest, it was Jesus who revealed the true heart of His Father.

11 Slaughtering innocents to appease an angry god is a pagan custom, not a heavenly requirement.

12 And like the original Passover Lamb, it is the blood of Jesus that keeps the slayer away from our door, while the high priest is nowhere to be seen.

13 It is written *"My house shall be a house of prayer for all nations"* but the high priest wouldn't let anyone else in, and rather than for prayer, they ran it as the nation's abattoir.

14 And as regards the sacrifice of innocent creatures, people who think taking life will please the 'Giver of all life' are slapping Him in the face.

15 Should anyone be thinking of Aaron as being a good example, he, by providing the golden calf, quickly led the people astray, resulting in many deaths; high priests have followed their father's example ever since.

16 Who can the high priest represent more than the serpent – slaughtering countless innocent lambs, innocent saints, and crucifying the Lamb of God?

17 The most dangerous place for Jesus was in Jerusalem.

18 The most dangerous place for His flock was in Jerusalem. The most dangerous place for the Reformers was in Rome.

19 When are God's children going to wake up to the dangers surrounding religious leaders and religious places?

20 But such warnings are abhorrent to the viper's brood.

48 The Old-time Christian religion was strict; back then, a Christian seen drinking in a pub, was backslidden.

2 The Charismatic Movement introduced more freedom, and the seed sown from it demonstrates this.

3 We now have wine, beer and spirit drinking church-going, and church-leading people, within Christianity.

4 But can we encourage the unbeliever to leave his lifestyle while we are enjoying it with him?

5 Our God is a Miraculous God; everything He does is a miracle, and the proof of the presence of the

Miracle God is the miracle, not the ability to tutor, or to preach, or the loud music.

6   Spiritual growth leads to spiritual maturity, for which each individual has a calling.

7   The true Christian life is a journey of discovery of getting to know God, through Jesus Christ His Son; it is costly in many ways, mostly in our time.

8   Of the only two places to spend eternity, one is with God in His kingdom of truth, light and life, the other is without Him, in eternal chaos, darkness and death; we choose here and now, which?

9   Children come to understand their parents only as they grow up; therefore, God's children who do not yet understand Him, have yet to grow up.

10 With its confidence and dependency, child-like innocence always brings from the heart of God a loving, father-like response.

11 For all the children of God, the 'cutting off all-round', the 'separation from' or the 'rejection of' their sinful nature, while still spiritual babies, is the true biblical circumcision.

12 The Holy Spirit is mother-like in the way She keeps cleaning, correcting and encouraging Her children.

13 The last thing disobedient children want is the correction they most need; to this, we all nod agreeably until we realise that we are the children.

14 Instead of reading *'the greatest in the kingdom'* read *'the most important in the kingdom'*, this may help us to see that Jesus was speaking about the least of His brethren, the children who believe in Him; not the outstanding nor the famous.

15 Each time we gather, we tell ourselves that Christ is in our midst, but there is little evidence of Him.

16 Man is incapable of discerning between, the *life* offered in the gentle hand of God, and the *knife* in the hard fist of Satan.

17 To all men, Jesus said, *"Come! Follow Me!"* He did not say, work hard and support those who follow Me.

18 There is no alternative for any man but to follow Jesus for himself.

19 Jesus does not need to intercede between man and God; He and His Father both love us equally.

20 His intercession involves standing face to face with the slayer, eyeball to eyeball so to speak, and saying, "To get to My people, you must deal with Me first." That is the only reason why we remain safe.

49 Standing by the side of religious people, means unbelievers swipe all of us with the same paintbrush.

2 Thus unbelievers will be unable to distinguish the spiritual from the ritual, the true Doorway from the false.

3 By not teaching them where they came from, and how painful it was to get here, the Protestant churches have failed God's children miserably.

4 After the very high price paid for its freedom, now lukewarm, the church sleeps!

5 Any imported psalm, so-called truth or health-ritual from another religion, cannot benefit the Christian one iota.

6 Religion, in all its guises, is the biblical mother of harlots.

7 Man has no window through which he can look and observe heaven.

8 From within our physical environment, we have no way of seeing, hearing, touching, smelling or tasting anything that is in the spiritual realm.

9   Unless spiritual beings choose to reveal themselves to us, we remain completely deaf, blind and ignorant of them.

10 Being inside this physical 'envelope' is comparable to being a baby in the womb, alive, but having no conception of what lies ahead or outside.

11 Until we pass through, from here to there, it is not possible for us to truly grasp or experience the true spiritual environment. Biological capabilities do not interact with the spiritual environment. If God communicates clearly with us it is usually through visions or dreams.

12 True *servants* of Jesus do not defend their position of authority because, regarding those they serve, *servants* do not have any. We should remember this if we desire to be great in the kingdom.

13 With so much leisure-time available today, the god of entertainment has a very powerful pull on our hearts and minds.

14 With the idols we provide for them, our children are especially vulnerable.

15 It is difficult for me to think of a more impressive and more powerful, lying-miracle, or a better description of a household idol, than TV.

16 Anyone prepared to lie to you, given the chance, will also steal from you to obtain what he or she covets.

17 Idols are thieves; they steal our fruit and we remain, or else we become, barren.

18 The little tykes are so efficient that they will take from us even that which we thought we could never lose, and like Rachel, we sit on them and pretend we have none.

19 God does not reclaim any blessings – our idols steal them, stunt our spiritual growth and in the end will leave us destitute.

20 In the presence of idolatry, achieving holiness, a close walk with God, and bearing fruit for Him, is not possible; idolatry is rampant in Christianity, as it was in Israel.

50 To birth His eternal children, God has chosen cleanliness as being essential for those scattering His seed.

2 Christians are the light of the world, only if they shine with the light of the Light of the World.

3 He has chosen generosity instead of greed, love instead of hate, compassion instead of indifference and humility instead of pride.

4 And to show exactly who does the works, He chooses inability instead of capability.

5 Setting out without preparation, means the Holy Spirit must teach us on the road.

6 This appeals to many eager beavers, but it can be hazardous, especially for those who believe our half-truths, accept our dodgy advice and repeat our incomplete or confusing messages.

7 It is not possible for those who are immature to teach without adding to or taking away from the message.

8 The answer, "I don't know, but one day all will become clear." comes from immaturity. "I do not know but I will ask God and find out" comes from a growing Christian.

9 Disciplining other people, while still under tuition, is very hazardous; it is trying to remove specks out of their eyes while having planks in our own.

10 The very word *elder*, by definition, refers to growth, not appointment.

11 We can ignore them, but we can neither appoint nor dismiss true spiritual elders, because their spiritual growth makes them such; Jesus chooses His servants!

12 The Church of Jesus Christ is not a democracy!

13 Fellowshipping regularly provides ample opportunity to exercise all the gifts and ministries within the church naturally, under the supervision of the Holy Spirit, but there is no chance of this happening in programmed services because leaders cannot dictate when God can speak.

14 Spiritual gifts can be exercised perfectly, unforced, un-announced, and daily on cue, during genuine free Christian fellowship, worship and prayer.

15 However, it seems Christians cannot meet up as a group of friends; they usually make it a mini service.

16 The river from God can only ever be as pure as the container it passes through.

17 And to get in deep, one must first paddle.

18 Although others may not see our inner impurity, it still has its contaminating effect on our words and behaviour.

19 No serious opposition proves the serpent thinks we are unlikely to tread on it.

20 'Spiritual *nakedness*' refers to having no righteous robe. Unbelievers, startled and embarrassed at seeing our nakedness, keep their distance, laugh at us, or shake their heads and look the other way.

51 No matter how desperate or justified it may appear, asking for finances to support one's ministry is un-scriptural.

2 Like beggars, evangelists and pastors have become both skilled and persistent in asking for money to run their businesses.

3 *"Dead works"* is the name given to any kind of word, task, ministry or help, carried out by the old sinful nature in its attempt to work for God.

4 Struggling, in our strength, produces dead works.

5 Religion is an organisation specifically designed by the religious spirit, for man to practice, teach and glory in dead works.

6 Our sinful nature hates humility, but loves dead works; they give it a sense of being righteous, and a good way to earn God's favour.

7 If ever anyone fired blanks, it is the Christian busy in dead works.

8 Jesus said, *"Of Myself, I can do nothing"* and neither can we; when we try, it produces dead works.

9 If Satan thinks you have any time for God, then he will keep you busy by pushing more dead works and distractions in your direction to encourage you to work harder.

10 Busy lives, inside or outside a church, is a sure sign that a man or woman is neglecting Jesus.

11 Provided the serpent can keep us busy under the authority of someone else, and away from private prayer, we will remain powerless against it.

12 The statement, "Busy working for God" is most likely to mean up-to-the-neck in dead works.

13 The apostle's reference to dead works involves *'repentance from'* them.

14 Dead works being just *"an elementary principle"* is almost unbelievable today; especially considering the vast majority of Christendom is still producing lorry-loads of the stuff.

15 The decision to sit out front on the platform, or attend the Pastors Conference or the Leaders Seminar is deliberately to distinguish those who think they have, from those who they think have not.

16 Popular playground games often include pretence; pretence is another word for hypocrisy.

17 "Lord, save us from the talkative" is the silent prayer of those uncomfortable and suffering under the excess of words from the politician and the preacher.

18 Not everyone can preach, and not everyone that can preach knows when to shut up and sit down.

19 Even those who are silent have an opinion, and maybe a worthwhile suggestion.

20 But if we wish to hear what those who are slow to speak have to say, then we have to shut up because those that stutter, or hesitate before speaking, require silence and patience from everyone else.

52 Hypocrisy makes one an ineffective witness to the resurrection of Jesus Christ because, instead of representing Him, unknowingly, we represent ourselves.

2 Who we *claim* to be, is of little value; other people, especially unbelievers, have a much clearer view of who we are.

3 Due to our eagerness to labour for God, we often have difficulty in grasping, firstly – that we of ourselves can do nothing, and secondly that without Jesus we are nothing.

4 The angel of the Lord ripped open the Temple Veil for a completely different reason than to permit access by lukewarm Christians.

5 The Holy Bible has been, and still is today in some nations, a very costly book to publish, distribute and own; for many, the price they pay is their life.

6 Buy a Bible while you still can, and read it prayerfully while you still have the opportunity.

7   Due to its value in our spiritual education, the Holy Spirit uses large portions of Scripture as parables.

8   The Jew, Christian or atheist will understand Scripture according to the shepherd they follow, whoever he or she may be.

9   The Bible habitually and regularly mentions truth, but it does so without explaining it.

10 God did not provide Scripture as a shepherd for His children, for that important task, He gives His Holy Spirit.

11 Being unprepared to tolerate another opinion, always results in people standing on different foundations, building different churches.

12 Being unprepared to tolerate another opinion, also reveals a lack of confidence in what we do believe.

13 Being unprepared to tolerate a different opinion makes a person or a church a 'closed shop'.

14 If we insist on calling the Bible "God's Word" then the only way we, as Christians, will be able to stay united in what we believe, is to keep things very, very simple, and not go any deeper. In this situation, to maintain unity, milk must remain our only food.

15 More, deeper, further and higher with God, is always different, and anything different is unacceptable to those who accept only their agreement as permissible, and insist upon it for unity.

16 Accompanying any idea to jump off a pinnacle, or any prompt to step out of a boat, is the unconscious desire to be noticed; and whispered scripture from behind is a push.

17 Any voices, real or imagined, quoting what seem to be appropriate passages of scripture in our everyday lives, may not necessarily be from, or with the blessing of the Holy Spirit. Children play games!

18 The apostle Paul was a tentmaker, not a farmer, so forget *adoption* and *grafting*; we are children of God through *birth*, or we have no family relationship with Him whatsoever.

19 Jesus taught that unless we are *born again* of the Spirit of God we would never even see the kingdom.

20 The Seed of life comes from the Father, not from any substitute. The Creator God is a Father only to those who are *born* of His Spirit!

53 Naturally, education is available through studying books; spiritual education is not.

2 To bear a holy word requires holiness; quoting scripture aloud is not speaking God's Word.

3 All religions, including Christianity, are democratic organisations; the kingdom of God is not.

4 The saying, "Power corrupts, and absolute power corrupts absolutely" is not quite true; it is more truthful the other way round, to say, the corrupt seek power, and the absolutely corrupt seek absolute power.

5 Worldly eyes see only worldly views of spiritual events; they only see the parable and not the truth within it.

6 Naming buildings, grottos and carpets and other things as being holy, will encourage idolatry.

7 Mention holy ground and we automatically look down at the floor.

8 Mention holy places and we glance around at the walls.

9 While ever the serpent can maintain our eyes and attention on that created or built, instead of the Creator, and upon the field and its fence, instead of the horizon, then it can stir up covetousness to claim it, and hatred and war to possess it.

10 Religious leaders take the truth, and by claiming they have authority to interpret it, introduce their ideas, first alongside the truth, then swamping the truth, and finally as a replacement of the truth.

11 Gradually these ideas are modified and twisted further until any resemblance of truth is lost. The result is people who do not know the truth teaching the exact opposite of the truth, as being the truth, to people who cannot tell the difference.

12 Interestingly, the thorns and thistles in Adam's curse could include religion, for it springs up wherever man sows his seed; it increases his burden, chokes his seed, spoils his fruit and blocks his path.

13 Once a religion establishes political control, it instigates strict laws to enforce compliance to it, and administers severe retribution to anyone opposing it; read Church History and observe Islamic nations.

14 During revivals, people with natural understanding and abilities, step in as spiritual leaders and teachers, take over and replace previous styles of religious control, for a similar one.

15 No matter how wide their smile, how fine their robes, or how intellectual and persuasive their speeches, it is still extremely dangerous to submit to religious leaders.

16 Even loving and praying for them is dangerous; do not follow them.

17 Rather than shake their hand, Jesus confronted religious leaders; He did not submit to their presumed authority.

18 He called them "Hypocrites", "Fools" "Blind guides that strain at a gnat and swallow a camel" and "Brood of vipers", and asked them, "How can you escape the condemnation of hell?"

19 Restrictive comments and rules provided by religious people, come from a desire to anesthetise you, nail your feet to their floor, and keep you inside their walls supporting them, until, lifeless, they bury you in their churchyard.

20 Follow no religious leader; follow only Jesus!

54 During the time they spent with Jesus, the disciples would have heard far more truth, absorbed far more light and experienced considerably more of the kingdom than the vast majority of today's Christians experience in a lifetime.

2 The one certainty about libraries, sermons and well-meaning advice, is that they all contain mountains of supposition.

3 The world's traditional method of educating its children through the printed word, visual aids and oral lecturing is an extremely poor provider of truth, but an excellent source of error

4 The need for Jesus to call us, prepare us, and send us, is in everyone's best interest, not least our own.

5 But the heart of man is deceitful above all things and desperately wicked, and when men say, "Thus says the Lord..." we put our eternal life in jeopardy if we believe them outright.

6 Listen and observe his behaviour, before accepting a man as your Christian brother.

7 To first observe their fruit is wise, not disrespectful.

8 As a loving father, God deals with His children as individuals, not in groups; this is especially so with tuition.

9 If I have a living relationship with Jesus, as my Rabbi, why do I need a teacher? If Jesus is my shepherd, then why do I need a pastor?

10 And God needs a prophet only for speaking to wayward children who are ignoring Him.

11 Therefore, the prophet is only God's second-best way of communicating with His children; by which time He is usually desperate to save them.

12 As with any loving father, His primary choice is a loving, personal, one-to-one intimate relationship with His children.

13 Truly, Jesus will not forsake us, but we must not forsake Him,

14 But subtlety accomplishes easily what the crowbar, club and whip find impossible.

15 Rather than frown upon a different opinion, seeing it as an opportunity for contention, we can and should expect them, even enjoy them.

16 Unity is not each member seeing things the same way, nor is it agreeing to do the same things.

17 Unity among God's people is all being members of the same Body, obedient to the same Head.

18 God will most likely be saying different things to each individual.

19 Lest we covet them, God does not direct our eyes towards other people's belongings, but the enemy does.

20 Gifts from God, great or small, never involve breaking any of the Ten Commandments to acquire them. How does the conquest of Canaan look in this light? Think about that!

55 We will not survive our journey, through our wilderness, by eating only what the world offers us.

2 The laws mentioning clean and unclean foods are parables about this.

3   Both the Jew and the Christian, consume vast quantities of unclean food, of which entertainment is a major source on the high street, in every living room, and these days even in our pockets.

4   If we desire to grow in righteousness then we should not consume the kind of food the world is eager to provide for us, and after which our sinful nature lusts.

5   Healthy children have healthy appetites, and our hunger for truth proves to the God of truth that we desire Him.

6   If we spend so little time and effort seeking the presence of Jesus now, and if we have so little desire to get to know Him more intimately now, what makes us think that God will choose such cold, indifferent, unfaithful whores as a Bride for His Son?

7   There is a good chance many people calling themselves Christian, may fall far short of their expectations, simply by their lack of love for Jesus in this life. If we love Him, then we will obey Him.

8   So, why should a Mercy Seat require blood sprinkling on it? As a *receipt* for the purchase of this entire world and everyone in it, that's why!

9   Persecutions are nothing new, but intense, continuous and amazing distractions are.

10 The world harvest being ripe includes ripe tares as well as ripe wheat; wickedness will intensify towards the end, as it now seems to be doing.

11 God loves all His children, those who know, as well as those who have yet to find out.

12 The disciples failed to cast out a spirit from a lad, but they went to their Tutor to ask Him why.

13 When what we try to do for people fails, why do we not follow their example?

14 Tutors teach and commission their students; such students should go to their tutors with their questions; Jesus won't answer them; He does not teach students of other tutors.

15 Each move of God brings with it new poetry, songs and style of worship.

16 But the songs and style of worship from a previous move of God do not seem to thrill those in a new move quite as much, and vice versa.

17 But God loves variety, even though we may not.

18 If Jesus had to personally teach His disciples yesteryear, then He will have to personally teach His disciples this year.

19 The cross is an implement of death, not a badge. In reality, do we wear one, instead of one wearing us?

20 While kneeling repentant at the foot of His cross, Christ enters our life, but once nailed to our cross we then enter into His.

56 A false claim to be a child of God, is blasphemy, and probably another way to take His name in vain?

2 The serpent said, "Has God really said...?" And thinking they would be wise, like God, they swallowed the lie, hook, line and sinker, and died.

3 False prophets today, say, "Genesis is just a story, scientists have proven the earth to be billions of years old; only six thousand years old? Don't be silly!" And Christians swallow the lie; hook line and sinker, thinking they are wise, like God.

4 Jesus overcame this world, with its wicked ruling authorities, without using violence.

5 He expects all His people to overcome this world in the same way; only those who overcome will warrant His reward.

6   Power to overcome the world is not the ability to subdue and control those dwelling in it. God does not give men authority over other men.

7   The power that overcomes the world is humility, and submission only to God, not to worldly authorities.

8   Jesus overcame this world by refusing to yield to any authority running it; He was submissive only to His Father God.

9   Living righteously is essential, but it is not *preaching* the Gospel, and neither is telling sinful people that God loves them.

10 For salvation, we are supposed to leave our filth, wash, and then enter His purity. He is not supposed to leave His purity and join us in our filth.

11 Jesus mixed with harlots and tax collectors, yes, but not on their terms; they came repenting of their sin and washed clean from it, to Him; He was their Lord!

12 'Unconditional love' is not a Biblical principle, but rather, sinful human nature trying to convince itself that God loves it.

13 The sinner turns away from his sin, unto God, or he remains guilty of it.

14 The problem is that men can turn away from doing what was wrong, to do something else that may seem better, but is still wrong; repentance from sin must be unto God for salvation. Being sorry you were caught is not being sorry that you did it!

15 If I hide iniquity in my heart then God will not even listen to me.

16 Wisdom is the river of life, it only flows when there is somewhere for it to flow to.

17 A man's hunger for wisdom will draw it from God; therefore, we could say, God's children have their hands on His tap.

18 The Holy Spirit only speaks if we are listening, and unless He has freedom, keeps silent anyway.

19 Give to the dead and what you give is dead.

20 Give to the dead only what will lead them towards life.

57 Those following Jesus Christ must pass through the water with Him before entering their wilderness.

2 I suspect that there are some laws within the Bible that I do not keep; of some I am unaware, and some I might dismiss as inappropriate anyway.

3 If there are laws within the Holy Book that I do not keep, then how can I quote other laws from the Holy Book and expect my neighbour to keep them? The beam in my eye blinds me.

4 The need of every soul is a personal relationship with the Lord Jesus Christ; from within that relationship, He will show each how He wants them to live.

5 He upholds everything, or it collapses. He supports everything, or it falls over. He feeds us, or we starve. He gives life, or we stay dead.

6 Such is our amazing God that everything within Him wants to give, help and support. His amazing character means all we have to do is welcome Him, yield to His authority and accept His help.

7 He could not have made things any easier for people in this Creation or for angels in any of His previous Creations, which I accept there have been many throughout eternity.

8 The Ten Commandments were not the test that God set for Israel; they were a standard for Jesus to prove He is righteous, which He did.

9 Our test is simply to seek Him each day for truth, to grow up in His image and in His likeness, and *remember* to acknowledge Him by fellowshipping

with Him on the Sabbath. Sabbath means rest, not bondage!

10 How important is seeking God daily for wisdom – for our share of Manna?

11 Solomon was a wise man; obediently, he arose before the sun each morning to gather his wisdom from God.

12 Regardless of whether we accept the test set by God for His people, we should at least acknowledge its value.

13 The need for men to seek God for His truth must surely be unquestionably beneficial.

14 So, how important is keeping the Ten Commandments? Well, how important is it to obey God?

15 By the Fourth beginning with the word *"Remember..."* it is clear that God desires we do not forget it! And leave at least that day free each week, to fellowship with Him.

16 Signs are to confirm the messenger and his message as coming from God; remove the messenger and his message and the signs disappear.

17 *"The older shall serve the younger"* He meant, *"The greater shall serve the lesser."*

18 God's word to Rebekah was an instruction, rather than a prophecy.

19 Jesus said, *"Whoever desires to become great among you, let him be your servant."*

20 Stepping out to do battle in the name of Jesus of Nazareth, when not sent, is another way to take His name in vain; remember Ai!

58 Disrespect splits families, and friends, and causes wars.

2 By heeding sensitive Sarah, Abraham rejected his wife, Hagar, and his son, Ishmael.

3 Rejection is a sore and difficult wound to heal; it lingers a long time.

4 Evidence of that same wound is still obvious today, even more so today.

5 The blessing of God includes multiplication.

6 Jesus broke the bread and the fishes to begin this process.

7 While ever they kept breaking the bread it kept multiplying.

8 The food only stopped multiplying when they stopped breaking it.

9 Judgement will be by observation; what a man has grown up to become, and not by recalling the past.

10 Recalling the past seems unlikely since memories about clay things, stored in clay minds, in clay brains, within clay vessels, will all have perished in clay.

11 The Holy Spirit is Life. Blaspheme Her and you reject the life She gave you; this is unforgivable.

12 If you want to keep life and live long in the Land, then respect the One who gave life to you.

13 Do not reject God if you value what He provides.

14 *"Then He lifted up His eyes toward His disciples, and said, 'Blessed are you poor, for the kingdom of God is yours.'"*

15 Stop considering the competent as being the most important; value the weakest.

16 Stop praising and supporting the achiever; comfort, help and support those struggling.

17 If a man does not know Jesus, then from a relationship point of view, Jesus does not know that man.

18 The Law keeps sinners outside the camp, but Jesus goes out there to find, comfort, heal and bring them to repentance to save them.

19 Love is closer to 'works' than it is to 'faith'.

20 If the way we behave reveals the things that we truly love, then what we truly love will influence our behaviour – one may need to think about that.

59 Today, we abound with knowledge; but spiritual truth is scarce, and probably always has been.

2 Your children are borrowing your faith if they are not asking you questions about it, and they will leave it behind with you when they leave home.

3 Failing to ask our Father God questions, shows we too are borrowing the faith of another, perhaps that of our friends or our church, if so, then we are likely to leave it behind when we leave our house.

4 Worship without righteousness is an abomination to the Lord.

5 Woe to those at ease in a time of unrighteousness!

6 Men can easily remove righteousness, but they cannot put it back.

7 Praying, preaching or testifying will not restore righteousness in the land.

8 God alone can restore righteousness!

9 Only when we *"Who are called by His name, humble ourselves and pray and seek His face, and turn from our wicked ways, will God hear from heaven, forgive our sin and heal our land."*

10 An important part of repentance involves turning away from the leaders we have chosen, back to following only Jesus; otherwise, we will remain unfaithful and continue to stray.

11 The quiet, laid-back person finds waiting on God much easier than the competent, industrious, extrovert.

12 The hesitant falter when facing the same challenges that thrill others; there can be serious problems, as well as enormous blessings, for both.

13 Rather than one way or the other being correct, God individually leads each individual.
14 We are not pre-programmed machines; He does not take us by the scruff of our necks and drag us along a particular path we detest.
15 He will not demand the extrovert sits quietly at the back *too* early, nor will He force the introvert to the front *too* soon.
16 To this day, my observations have shown me that whether we 'wait' or 'work', whether we 'stay' or 'go' it has little effect on the world.
17 In truth, all those who do go, leave a mission field full of very needy people behind them, and weaken the church in the process.
18 Each individual may learn and grow while doing their own thing, in their way, for Jesus, with Jesus; but do not claim He sent you if He did not!
19 Respecting each other will mean acknowledging that each has a right to take the path they believe Jesus is leading them.
20 Moses was right; we do what seems right in our own eyes; but this may not be wrong, just childlike!

60 The only Gospel some people will ever read is the Gospel according to you!
2 Through our lives, we all preach a continuous and silent message to unbelievers, and by doing so, we reveal the One whom we serve.
3 Faith should be based, not on the *ability* to move the mountain, but rather that Jesus has given you the *authority* to move the mountain.
4 Faith should be based, not on the *ability* to tread on serpents, but rather that Jesus has given you *authority* to tread on serpents.

5   Faith should be based, not on the *ability* to rebuke cancer, but rather that Jesus has given you the *authority* to rebuke cancer.

6   If we are not careful, then our faith will stand on our level of faith, rather than on the absolute authority of Jesus.

7   Once given authority, faith is almost irrelevant – mustard seed size even.

8   When Jesus gives authority, miracles are easy.

9   By definition, a 'Christian' accepts Jesus Christ as Lord, and everything He taught as being the absolute truth.

10 The one's doubting what Jesus taught were the religious scribes, Pharisees and chief priests – those who wanted Him dead.

11 People unwilling to believe Moses, when confirmed by Jesus, are fake Christians.

12 While ever I am following my Shepherd then He does not need to keep informing me when to turn left or right, I just keep following Him.

13 However, if I go before Him, then for me to obey His wishes, He must keep shouting His instructions from behind me.

14 The former is easy, the latter fraught with problems because there are many voices shouting "This way! Not that!"

15 Constrained only by righteousness and a little wisdom, I seem free to do almost anything and go almost anywhere I like.

16 The way only seems narrow to those who would rather be off it.

17 If inquisitive and we ask Jesus questions, His answers will solve problems, feed us, thrill us, and lead us towards maturity.

18 Without questions, answers are meaningless.

19 A belief that you have the authority of Jesus to minister to others, miraculously, is easily testable.

20 Open your front door and look outside; the length of the queue there, waiting to receive miraculous help, is directly proportional to the heavenly power you possess.

61 Dead people do not go to heaven; those with life do not go to hell.

2 Biological *life* is part of this Creation; it is not eternal.

3 Grasp this; regarding goodness, righteousness and faithfulness, God is very reliable, and therefore, very predictable!

4 God desires we give and receive, not out of ignorance but with understanding, lest we later regret giving, and accuse Him of taking what was ours.

5 Our verbal promises to God carry little weight because, as His children, we are prone to changing our mind, or even forgetting what we promised Him in the first place.

6 Anger, hate and covetousness are signs of intended violence; Jesus warns of the consequences if we entertain any of them.

7 Violence is one way to suppress, oppress, and conquer or repossess, un-righteously.

8 Whatever promises the wedding vows may or may not contain, it is God who instigated marriage and specified the conditions. Politicians need to acknowledge this.

9 From wherever we are, we grow from the state of *being* wrong to a condition of *being* right, and we may view this change rightly, as growing up.

10 Just as in the natural, growing up spiritually is slow and almost imperceptible.

11 Nevertheless, no matter how slow, God must change us, or else...!

12 Our populating heaven, exactly as we are, would change it from being heavenly, where all is neat and sweet, to being earthy, where all is crime and grime.

13 The Church sleeps because it is no longer excited with Jesus.

14 Like Adam, his children fail because we are immature, naïve, and vulnerable against a mature, deceptive enemy suggesting the fruit of disobedience is tasty and will make us wise like God.

15 I agree with others that the principle of life seems to be, no birth without pain and no freedom without a fight.

16 God, observing this selfish world, has decided that in His kingdom "there will be no crown without a cross."

17 One cannot keep the gift and refuse the giver of the gift; rejecting the Holy Spirit means rejecting life.

18 Forgiveness is not possible when the One who forgives has been rejected.

19 The world is gathering against God's children to annihilate them, but not clothed in armour, driving tanks with guns blazing.

20 Armageddon is a battle to kill, not so much physically, but through entertaining the soul.

62 We have left our First Love; we are sacrificing our children to the god of entertainment.

2 While thinking we are rich, we are poor, blind and wretched.

3 Our Saviour views our lukewarm condition as abhorrent.

4 We have a form of godliness but this is only an outer show, inside our heart, and in our pockets and homes, we store and treasure our idols.

5   In our current condition we may speak well of Jesus, but does Jesus speak well of us?

6   Jesus said to His disciples, *"If they believed Me then they will believe you!"*

7   He said the same the other way round, *"If they do not believe you, then they would not believe Me."*

8   And that was a reliable rule-of-thumb for them to assess others. But we must remember, He was speaking to His disciples speaking His word, not to us speaking ours.

9   Anyone refusing to accept what Jesus taught has not accepted Jesus as Lord.

10 I conclude that it is not *all* right to trust God in all circumstances, but only all right to trust Him if what we are doing, or what we are about to do, is *all* right.

11 The difference between when He speaks and when we speak is that His word is almighty; ours is very weak and suspect.

12 Children love to play games. Pretentious games involve hypocrisy; point this out to children, and it spoils their game and they walk away from you sullen.

13 We use our hands for many things, one of them is when giving, but we cannot give anything if our hands are empty.

14 Peter and John held sufficient in their hands to make the lame man leap for joy.

15 What do we have in our hands? If nothing, then do not play pretentious games.

16 God is the only one who can restore our nation; He alone builds His Church, and He alone can restore righteousness in the land. Our feeble attempts amount to dead works and religious games.

17 God's answer to our problems, begins something like, *"If My people, who are called by My name..."*

18 Those who believe they are doing right, tend to criticise those whom they think are doing wrong, which is something which humility and the love of forgiving others, softens.

19 Love and humility soften any tendency to condemn the sinner.

20 On that Day, many condemned by men will receive life from God, and many praised by men, destruction.

63 Beware; all preachers are salesmen!

2 Must the flames see Jesus in our midst, to refrain from roasting us?

3 Must the lions that we encounter see Jesus by our side before they will forego their lunch?

4 Perhaps we require Him by our side before making a stand against the enemy, and before victory becomes a certainty – remember Ai!

5 Are we offering our lives to God, to receive what He offers?

6 If we are, then does the God of love delight in such transient faithfulness?

7 To prove the quality of our relationship and faithfulness, we must dwell for a time outside of that 'Secret Place', outside His protection and blessings, exposed to trouble and pain – remember Job!

8 Only faithfulness and love through bad times prove faithfulness and love.

9 The Bible abounds with advice for men to fear God, but why should I fear Him?

10 How does one fear the God who is love?

11 The thing I must fear is *me* not loving *Him*!

12 God watches and records our words and actions, especially those made behind closed doors because that is where we are least hypocritical.

13 Hypocrisy permeates Christianity as much as any other religion.

14 Tell God that you can see and He will not open your eyes. And if the vessel believes itself to be clean and full, then He cannot clean and fill it.

15 Christians are not as quick to *"Go, sell all that you have and give it to the poor"* as we may be to claim, *"Whatsoever you ask in My name, I will do it."*

16 Covetousness is very selective!

17 God provides scripture for our education, not as our shepherd.

18 Followers, especially part-time followers, do not qualify as disciples of Jesus.

19 Our faithfulness to Jesus undergoes its most severe test when likeable, competent people offer to pastor, teach and lead us.

20 Our words are not the words of God any more than the noise from sheep bleating in the fields are the words of the shepherd. [That's a good one Lord!]

64 Accepting the Seed of the Gospel of Jesus Christ may be nearer to our *conception* than to our *birth.*

2 Leadership is not by the visible presence of God, His frequent verbal directions or by His finger writing on the wall.

3 Father God leads His young children, figuratively speaking, as they cling to His skirts, listen to what He says and observe what He does.

4 However, He does expect them to grow up without crutches to lean on, or skirts from which to hang.

5 Problems arise when, as children, we let go of His skirt to cling to the garments of others. We may still grow up, but it will be in their image and likeness and not in His.

6 Such Christians will stand as individuals, firm in what they believe but unable to think as God thinks, say what He says or recognise what He does.

7 Gentiles are undisciplined, which shows itself in the way we pick and choose from the Commandments, which to obey.

8 This viewpoint reveals the covetous heart as it claims all the promises, without fulfilling any of the conditions.

9 The vast majority of Christians do not follow Jesus wherever He goes, but instead, tend to head in the general direction, in which they believe He went, which is not quite the same thing.

10 All church services, sermons, worship times, Bible studies, tuition courses, conferences, seminars and even Sunday Schools are a *waste of time* if the head of the house has no bread, directly from God, to feed his family.

11 With a flimsy excuse, one can break the strongest Commandment.

12 And the same flimsy excuse can silence a nagging conscience; but not so a tradition, to break a tradition takes great determination.

13 Israel rested on the promises given to their forebears; Christians habitually do the same. That is worth thinking about!

14 If I desire to enter His kingdom, then clinging to promises He gave to other people could be unreliable.

15 Trusting in any promise is unreliable if one does not know the one who made the promise.

16 Our behaviour towards others determines God's behaviour towards us.

17 God is meek and lowly in heart! But disregard a man's claim to be chosen by Him, and that man is liable to pick up stones to stone you.

18 To meet Jesus, we must leave filthiness behind, for Jesus will not abandon purity to join us in our filth.

19 The instruction God gave, *"You be holy because I AM holy"* could be the same as – do unto others whatever you would like Me to do unto you.

20 Are we spiritual people, or worldly people who can think spiritually occasionally? [That's another good one Lord!]

65 The truth is mentioned in Scripture, but not explained; to explain and teach the truth to His children, God provides the Holy Spirit.

2 No one pleasing God need have any fear about not serving Him.

3 Perhaps those who believe they are serving God, should check that they are pleasing Him?

4 To avoid disappointing them, we should always check with those for whom we work that we do so according to their wishes; the same applies while serving Jesus.

5 Water washes away neither leprosy nor sin; except when obedient to God's prophet or the word of the King Himself, telling people to wash.

6 In my relationship with Jesus, I must conform to His wishes and His standard, rather than He to mine. He is not at my beck and call.

7 If we lose our joy for Jesus, then we may know Him, and know about Him, but our faces will show a lack of joy, so will our walk with Him, and the way we talk about Him.

8 The more joy we have, the less we will need entertainment. Selah!

9 In the kingdom of heaven, we may all be princes and princesses, but we cannot all be kings and queens.

10 A relationship with Jesus is more important than just believing in Him; one can live an independent, sinful life while believing, but not from within a relationship with Him.

11 Better to know God, without knowing His name, than it is to know His name, without knowing Him.

12 There is a vast difference, between hearing God speak, and believing that He has spoken.

13 How do we overcome? We overcome by the blood of Jesus, but unless we say 'no!' in all the right places, His blood will not save us.

14 Saying yes, in the wrong places could ensure we take a different route and end up in the pit.

15 While ever one maintains reverence and support for religious leaders, then one is quite safe in and among them; but truth enflames them; read church history, read the Bible; look at other world religions!

16 Truthful people only tell the truth.

17 Among the mixed multitude leaving Egypt to follow Moses to the Promised Land, were some violent people.

18 Beware, on hearing the good news, mixed multitudes press into the kingdom of heaven and among them are also some violent people.

19 Doers' often rebuke incapable people. Doers' are usually beggars that rebuke the same incapable people that support them.

20 The truth is clear and easy to understand; part truth is complicated and deadly.

66 Adam rejected the word of God, and took the advice of another; by doing so, he lost truth, light and life, and died, not physically, but spiritually.

2 Void of truth, in darkness and spiritually dead, Adam, from his fallen state, could only reproduce after his

own kind, that is, confused, disobedient, spiritually dead children.

3 Reproduction, of Adam's sinful, disobedient nature, has continued via his offspring ever since, not through women, but men!

4 Humanity's sinful nature passes to our offspring via the seed of men, not through the egg of the woman.

5 Jesus was born of a woman; He did not have Adam's sinful nature because God was His Father.

6 Some disapprove of men who are faithful to their wives, but who neglect Jesus.

7 Some disapprove of men who are faithful to Jesus, but who neglect their wives.

8 Men can expect disapproval from others, whichever path they take.

9 Enthusiasm for Jesus is surely a good thing to have. Enthusiasm will encourage faithfulness.

10 With enthusiasm for Jesus, will come the joy of the Lord.

11 The joy of the Lord would ensure we speak well of Him, with more emotion, and more convincingly.

12 Admiring glances towards idols, or ten minutes watching TV will remove the blessing, dampen our joy and enthusiasm for Jesus.

13 In the house of a violent man, there is violence!

14 God is meek and lowly in heart; He is never violent. If God were violent then there would be no devil around to oppose Him, and no sinner left alive to disobey Him; all sinners should already have realized this!

15 If violence formed part of God's character then this fearful characteristic would manifest itself in His household, with His approval; heaven would then be a violent place.

16 There is no violence in heaven; God is never wrathful or violent. Hallelujah!

17 Our Saviour holds the title, Prince of Peace; He, the Prince of Peace, is the Son of the GOD of Peace.

18 One of the most outstanding and individual characteristics of God Most High is that He *loves* to forgive, far more than to punish. Such a response is outside the scope of inflexible Laws written on stone.

19 Jesus informed His disciples *"Those who seek will find, to those who knock it will be opened, and those who ask will receive answers."*

20 But what we seek, whom we ask, and the door on which we knock will determine the path we walk and where it leads.

67 Believing that we are disciples of Jesus, leads us to believe our church is His Church and its ministers are His ministers; therefore, we think we should submit to them, believe them and support them. These logical assumptions lead millions into serious trouble.

2 Misuse of the word 'church' has led to calling religious buildings God's house, religious organisations Christ's Church, and their occupants God's children, when there is no guarantee God, Christ or His children have any real connection with any of them.

3 We have forgotten the Reformation, and the high price paid for our freedom by our spiritual forebears; we should not ignore Church History.

4 Church History proves that, provided they have the political power to do so, religious leaders will condemn, imprison and kill those opposing their claim to righteousness, truth, and to wield God's authority.

5 Like many religions, organised Christianity considers lies, persecution, cruelty and murder, as acceptable to fulfil its aims, people doubting this need to read Church History.

6 All and any injustice is permissible to a religion, providing it serves its interests.

7 Religion is still a dangerous beast, even when waving a Christian banner.

8 The Christian religion appears powerless today, only because it is fragmented, for this, we must thank God and the many who suffered to divide it.

9 Those working to reunite and empower Christianity are deceived; not understanding the dangers, they work for the enemy; and will prove to be the enemy!

10 Disapprove of their attempts to unite all religions, and they will condemn you.

11 *"Do unto others as you would have them do unto you"* is not in their rulebook or their heart.

12 It is unlikely that God created His angelic host pre-programmed for service, especially as we are currently undergoing trials and preparation to join them.

13 Perhaps the multitude of heavenly hosts all had their input into the creation of this world.

14 Perhaps by God involving them, He created according to their ideas and suggestions.

15 God works in partnership with His children!

16 We are not here just to do His bidding, but also to share the eternal life He has given to us, with Him.

17 This must mean co-operation with Him to a considerable degree, and such co-operation may well include some input in future Creations.

18 Mercy is an outstanding characteristic of God in heaven; He loves to forgive; therefore, those who are eager to forgive will be eagerly forgiven.

19 Mercy is righteous, whereas taking revenge is not. To punish is to retaliate and retaliation is wrong in life, as well as in football.

20 Man demands swift justice for lawbreakers while expecting leniency for his own offences.

68 According to the parable, no matter where the Gospel seed falls, it is its surroundings that dictate whether it will survive and fruit; the ball is in our court!

2 Humility is precious, for it will establish righteousness in a kingdom, a community, a family and even our own heart, without violence, which is why it has the blessing of God upon it.

3 Knowing the ways of the serpent, the wise man will only compliment another woman via her husband; and a wise woman, a man via his wife.

4 Self-acclamation reveals pride.

5 Witnessing of one's authority or value is a false witness; if we do this, then our own words confirm we are hypocrites.

6 One does not have to be a Caesar to think and behave as though he or she is God.

7 The instruction, *"The greater shall serve the lesser"* that God gave to Rebecca; Jesus gave to His disciples, because it means, in His kingdom the greatest shall care for the least, the strong for the weak.

8 Worshipping God behind closed church doors separates others, shutting them out; they then become strangers to us.

9 Being strangers' leads to suspicion, then distrust, and eventually to hatred and war.

10 Open communication and respect for my neighbour will prevent all that.

11 If we believe we are special and chosen of God, and tell our neighbour that he is not, then our neighbour will hate us.

12 God knew everyone while we were still in our mother's womb; there is nothing unique about this.

13 God did not breath life only into Adam; therefore, we should respect all flesh, two legs and four.

14 Living in a fleshy body, with our carnal nature, we deceive ourselves if we think we are in the image and likeness of God.

15 Speaking of making Man in Their image and after Their likeness, God was speaking of His Son Jesus.

16 At work or play, and even in the church, busyness will always crowd Jesus out of your life.

17 God sent Jesus to persuade us, rather than to threaten us; force is not an attribute of God.

18 God sent Jesus to rescue us, not to punish and drive us away.

19 Being meek and lowly in heart, God, the Master and Creator of the universe, seeks our friendship; therefore, now is the time to yield to Him! Today is the day for our salvation.

20 God first sent His Son Jesus at the right time in love, yes, but He promises to send Him later, again at the right time, for judgement.

69 Honour God, and give Him thanks for your every meal.

2 By speaking His word, God created everything we see around us; there are neither natural causes nor mathematical formulae that explain how God's word becomes reality; therefore, man will not find any; but there is a forest of imaginary trees for them to bark up, as they do!

3 Of itself, there is no power in the name of Jesus; many people bear this name. The power is God's authority that is behind the name.

4 Anyone not believing this can listen to children in the playground blaspheming His name without any conviction.

5 Scripture is complex; preachers compose many sermons from it, but revelation goes deeper.

6 God overcomes sadness with gladness.

7 He gives the silent a voice,

8 To the downcast a song.

9 Those bound, He sets free,

10 And to those tormented, peace and quietness.

11 He provides a clear spring for the thirsty.

12 He educates the ignorant!

13 To the lost, He reveals a path,

14 To the lonely, He provides a lifelong friend,

15 And for those meek and lowly in heart, He reserves a crown.

16 Sinners draw near to God, religious people think they are already near to God.

17 Wealth squandered by the Prodigal Son was unimportant; he lost a large portion of his life, which he could never regain.

18 After the destruction of the nation of Israel, the Scripture continues mentioning Israel because it is not speaking of Israel.

19 Every book has at least one chapter critical to the story – even the Apocrypha. Historically, parts of it follow the Old Testament, to speak of and to forecast what follows the New.

20 Since it holds information and prophecies of the period in which we live, unless we read the Apocrypha we will remain unaware of some future critical events.

70 With the authority God gave them it is highly likely that angelic beings run the kingdom of the heavens, watched over by their Father God. One day the apostles will join them.

2   Today, *wines* are always alcoholic drinks, but it is an error to assume the same applies to Scripture.

3   Both Eli and Hannah referred to drunkenness as wickedness – not just sin – but wickedness!

4   From being sober to being drunk is a sliding scale, where is the point of condemnation? Therefore, it is most likely that Jesus drank grape juice, not alcohol.

5   It is possible to mean well, but not do well.

6   To truly help someone is to provide what he or she needs, not what we think they need.

7   The path of ignorance includes living hungry in a time of plenty, failing to recognise the times, and being blind to snares on our path.

8   Forget His victory, or lose our joy, and we will hide, fearful of ridicule, persecution and defeat.

9   *"Let two or three prophets speak, and let the others judge what has been said."*

10 Inside or outside a religion, speakers are prophets, and the apostle's advice applies to them all, but check with your Shepherd before accepting any of it.

11 Respect also means listening to those who listen to us, talkative people struggle with this.

12 We should listen to what concerns others if we expect others to listen to what concerns us.

13 The educated classes stood to question Jesus; the poor fell at His feet. The former received rebukes, the latter healing, deliverance and life.

14 The scribes and Pharisees rejected the word of Jesus, even when surrounded by all the miraculous evidence He provided.

15 Today, scientists and teachers still reject the word of God, even surrounded by all the miraculous evidence God's spoken word provided.

16 We call it natural, but everything God does is a miracle.

17 Jesus said, *"Unless I wash you clean, there can be no fellowship between us."* Christians need to hear this because repentance and cleansing precede any fellowship with Him.

18 God is life! His word supports our every step, every heartbeat, every breath and every blink of the eye.

19 Originally, to sacrifice, meant giving of what you have until it hurt.

20 The false pen, twisted the word *sacrifice* to involve *shedding blood.*

71 To save the remnant, God had to destroy the nation!

2 Unless God shortens such days, then no flesh would be saved. Nebuchadnezzar served that purpose.

3 The people would leave the city, camp in the field, and then go to Babylon; going to Babylon saved them!

4 The people could not be delivered from their enemies without destroying the nation's corrupt, perverse authorities.

5 Once free from the corrupt leadership and its religion, God could bring them to repentance before returning them to rebuild their city. Selah!

6 Regarding temple sacrifices and the crucifixion of Jesus, religious men did both.

7 Shedding blood is sinful, especially when it is done in His name, and especially when it is His blood.

8 Common sense is not wisdom! Common sense is only the best we can do, and it differs from one to another.

9 God alone is wise; therefore, those without God have zero wisdom.

10 The Bible is an invaluable instruction book only if God is our Tutor, not men; otherwise, Scripture in the wrong hands is dangerous.

11 Jesus warned His disciples, *"The time is coming that whoever kills you will think he offers God service,"* and such wicked people get their guidance from another man's view of Scripture.

12 Jesus was the Rabbi for His disciples, and He is still the Rabbi for His disciples today.

13 If we desire to learn from Him, as opposed to countless others, then we must *spend* our time with Him, rather than with countless others.

14 Abraham married his half-sister. The apostle Paul, understanding this parable, said, *"Be not unequally yoked."* Paul, was advising young men to marry a daughter of their Father God but not a daughter of their mother i.e. to marry within the family of God.

15 The spiritual wilderness is a place where God deals with men and men deal with themselves before Him. Children enter this wilderness; only men and women of God come out of it.

16 Entertainment is the devil's substitute for the Joy of the Lord.

17 Come before Jesus meek and lowly in heart, not with your qualifications in your pockets and your abilities on your lips.

18 All that we are, and all that we have in this life, belongs here; this is why we can take nothing from it when we leave.

19 As well as being a dry, barren and hostile place, the wilderness is sometimes quiet and peaceful.

20 We must learn to trust God in the quiet and uneventful times as well as in the storms.

72 Mount Horeb was a dry, difficult place to get to, and a difficult place to be. Worshiping God on Mount Horeb proves you love Him.

2 Jesus said to the men He called, 'follow Me and I will teach you to fish for men.'

3 I would love to know what bait they used; I suspect the bait determines the type of fish caught.

4 Any bait that promises only benefits will attract one type, while that requiring repentance and the likelihood of persecution, another.

5 Every preacher seems to fish with different bait!

6 No man should accept what he cannot understand.

7 The teacher should not mention what he or she cannot explain simply and clearly to children.

8 Scripture rebukes Solomon because his foreign wives turned his heart; we should not be too hard on him, the hearts of many men have been turned by far less than 700 wives.

9 Even a wise man can become a fool, blamelessly, through some form of dementia in his old age.

10 And God will judge those who take advantage of people in such circumstances.

11 Men, being extremely poor leaders, lead others away from God and into unrighteousness by degrees.

12 The longer they lead others the further down the path towards destruction they take them.

13 "The greater shall *serve* the lesser!" Heaven functions on this principle and not on the greater *managing* the lesser.

14 If you claim to serve, do not attempt to manage. Servants do not manage those they serve.

15 Peter saw some of Paul's teachings as hard to accept; had Paul included them in his letters, other men

would have rejected those letters as being unsuitable for inclusion in the New Testament.

16 I am never frustrated if others refuse to walk my path, but I am puzzled as to why they expect me to walk theirs.

17 Only the Spirit filled prophet of God calling His people to repentance can prepare the way for Jesus to return.

18 To be truthful one must always be truthful. Telling a lie soils our garment.

19 Likewise, believing the truth means always believing what is true; accepting a lie also soils our garment.

20 We enslave ourselves by placing ourselves under the authority of another.

73 I heard somewhere that we do not have to lose ground to be disappointed; sometimes we just have to stay where we are.

2 The Church sleeps because it is no longer excited with Jesus.

3 Knowledge remains useless and fruitless outside of work.

4 Asking God, 'In the name of Jesus' is not a lever to force His hand. It describes a position – a place *in* Jesus.

5 Being *in* the name of Jesus Christ, equates to being *in* fellowship with Him, via His Holy Spirit.

6 The mission is to take Jesus to the lost and introduce Him; we cannot do this if we leave Him behind.

7 The idea is for Jesus to speak to them through us, and not for us just to talk to them about Him.

8 A belief in Scripture, as being the word of God, may encourage one to pick up the Book and go it alone.

9 Israel had no use for the supernatural gift of speaking in foreign languages, until Jesus sent His disciples to preach to the nations.

10 It appears that He chooses the most unlikely and incapable to do the most important and seemingly impossible tasks.

11 Truth is clear and easy to understand; part truth is complicated.

12 Idols must attract to survive. Even Christians advertise their idols by speaking well of them.

13 Perhaps fasting indicates difficult times, as well as being a way to end difficult times.

14 Do not misunderstand the meaning of 'humility' and 'servant-hood' to mean 'confidence' and 'leadership'.

15 Human nature views a servant of Christ as being in charge of the meal at which others dine, instead of serving at the meal at which others dine.

16 Human nature is not only *"Deceptive above all things and desperately wicked,"* but also very determined.

17 The sin of *presumption* is human nature's light-fingered attempt to take something that belongs to someone else.

18 *Faith* has an amazing ability to override common sense.

19 Human nature does not envy the servant, nor covet his job, but it does envy fame, success and leadership.

20 People, who do not understand, misunderstand.

74 God is respectful; therefore for *Him* to speak there must be freedom for *us* to speak.

2 Words spoken by men are not from God when there is no freedom for Him to speak.

3   The Bible warns us not to die in our sin; therefore, to save us, God must provide a *way* out of everyday sinning.

4   The salvation we speak of is the actual *route to righteousness*; day-by-day, step-by-step, we are *being saved* through our obedience to Jesus.

5   Salvation is a twofold event. Redemption through the blood of Jesus Christ, and purification by the Holy Spirit, it takes time and determination!

6   The Holy Spirit is not so much into answering our questions, as in teaching us His answers – there is a difference!

7   Who we are, determines what we do and what we do determines what we grow to become.

8   The church has a green light, until it turns red!

9   As effective as John the Baptiser was, he made no change to Jerusalem.

10 As effective as preachers may be, they all have no effect on religious centres.

11 Many people who have never seen the King, remain faithful to Him; God values such.

12 I think it wise for me to cling to the view that Jesus treasures me, for then I am more likely to treasure Him.

13 By always bearing in mind that I am treasure in His eyes, I am far more likely to view Him as treasure in mine, and appreciate Him and everything He does for me.

14 God is with me all the time; therefore, wherever I am, I should behave accordingly.

15 In Scripture, the word translated, as 'love' does not mean cuddles and kisses, but rather 'value and respect'.

16 Freedom is more easily recognisable, and experienced, when leaders are silent.

17 Praise God with your voice and worship Him with your life.

18 The scribes and Pharisees valued the scriptures higher than the One who provided them; we should not make the same mistake.

19 *"You have multiplied the nation but have not increased the joy. According to the harvest they rejoice before You, just the same as when dividing spoil."*

20 Do we rejoice and gave thanks, only according to the size of the harvest, or to the value of the spoil – only so long as things are going well?

75 There are some Christians who seek to please Jesus, and there are some Christians who seek Jesus to please them.

2 There are some Christians who ask Jesus what He wants them to do. And others that tell Him what they want Him to do.

3 Jesus is merciful and caring, but He is not at our beck and call!

4 Do not be surprised when others walk a different path.

5 Do not be surprised when they expect you to walk theirs.

6 By respecting our neighbour, our differences can become, not just interesting, but also exciting.

7 Jesus' instruction for unity involved the relationships between His disciples. It is impossible for His disciples to unite with religious people. History shows that religious people kill disciples of Jesus.

8 God reveals Himself through faith. Confidence in Him is the only way to see God.

9 It is right that we not only bear the name 'Christian' but also that in thought, in word and in deed, we are Christian.

10 For some, by calling themselves Christian, when they have no relationship with Christ, are using His name in vain.

11 By His word, GOD created the heavens and the earth in seven days, and by His word they will depart in seven days.

12 He that commanded men, not to lie, will never lie.

13 Likewise, He that commanded men not to kill, will never kill!

14 The one quick to speak is slow to listen.

15 That's like saying, he that speaks much, listens less; such people learn little.

16 Jesus is with those who are meek and lowly in heart.

17 We are justified by good behaviour, not by many words.

18 If one respects God, then he or she obeys His commandments.

19 Our nation's demise is the result of God's people choosing its leaders.

20 It is recorded that among many words there is always error; therefore, a wise man will say very little.

And with that, I hope by sharing all the above points from my journal, I have not overstepped the mark!